I0007887

CLOUD COMPUTING FOR BEGINNERS

A Comprehensive Guide

MAXWELL RIVERS

INTRODUCTION

In today's digitally-driven world, the term "cloud computing" has become increasingly prevalent in conversations about technology. It's not uncommon to hear businesses, tech enthusiasts, and even casual users discussing the cloud. But what exactly is cloud computing, and why does it matter? This book, "Cloud Computing for Beginners," aims to provide clear and accessible answers to these questions, making the world of cloud computing understandable and approachable for everyone.

What Is Cloud Computing?

At its core, cloud computing is a revolutionary paradigm that has transformed the way we think about computing resources. Gone are the days of storing all your data and running software on a single physical machine. Cloud computing allows you to harness the power of vast, distributed data centers spread across the globe. These data centers house an array of servers, storage devices, and networking equipment that can be accessed via the internet. Think of it as a vast, interconnected ecosystem of virtualized computing resources available on demand.

Why Cloud Computing Matters

Why should you care about cloud computing? The answer is simple: it has redefined the way we live and work. Whether you're a small business owner looking to scale your operations without massive upfront costs, a student collaborating on a group project, or an individual storing photos and documents online, cloud computing plays a vital role in your daily life. It offers unparalleled flexibility, scalability, and accessibility that traditional computing models simply can't match.

Who Should Read This Book

This book is tailored for beginners—those who may have heard of cloud computing but want to dive deeper into its concepts and practical applications. It's for business professionals seeking to understand how the cloud can enhance their operations, for students eager to explore the latest technology trends, and for anyone curious about the inner workings of the digital world around them. No prior technical knowledge is required; we'll start from the ground up and gradually build your understanding.

How to Use This Book

"Cloud Computing for Beginners" is structured to guide you through the fascinating world of cloud technology step by step. Each chapter will introduce key concepts, provide real-world examples, and offer practical tips to help you grasp the material. Whether you're reading cover to cover or jumping to specific topics of interest, this book is designed to be your friendly and informative companion on your cloud computing journey.

CONTENTS

1: UNDERSTANDING CLOUD COMPUTING

1.1 The Evolution of Computing

To truly grasp the significance of cloud computing, we must first take a step back and explore the fascinating journey that computing has undertaken over the years. The evolution of computing is a story of innovation, progress, and the relentless pursuit of making technology more accessible, powerful, and versatile.

From Abaci to Supercomputers: A Brief History

The roots of computing can be traced back to ancient civilizations, where devices like the abacus were used for arithmetic calculations. However, the true revolution began in the 19th century with the invention of mechanical calculators. These remarkable machines paved the way for automated computation and set the stage for the digital age.

The 20th century witnessed the birth of electronic computers, which marked a profound shift. Early computers, like the ENIAC (Electronic Numerical Integrator and Computer), were colossal machines that filled entire rooms. They were limited in processing power and required extensive manual programming.

As technology advanced, computers became smaller, faster, and more accessible. The development of microprocessors in the 1970s led to the rise of personal computers, making computing power available to individuals and small businesses. This era saw the emergence of household names like IBM, Apple, and Microsoft, who played pivotal roles in shaping the computing landscape.

The Internet Revolution

The 1990s brought another transformative force: the internet. It connected the world like never before and created new opportunities for sharing information and conducting business. The World Wide Web, invented by Tim Berners-Lee, democratized access to information and gave birth to the dot-com era.

During this time, companies began to realize the potential of the internet to deliver software and services remotely. The concept of Application Service Providers (ASPs) emerged, offering software over the web. However, these early attempts were limited by slow internet speeds and unreliable connectivity.

Birth of Cloud Computing

The true breakthrough came in the early 2000s with the advent of cloud computing. Companies like Amazon, Google, and Salesforce started to offer web-based services, paving the way for what we now know as Infrastructure as a Service (IaaS), Platform as a Service (PaaS), and Software as a Service (SaaS). Cloud computing transformed the way businesses operated by providing scalable, on-demand resources that could be accessed from anywhere with an internet connection.

Today, cloud computing is an integral part of our digital lives. It powers the apps on our smartphones, stores our photos and documents, enables remote work, and underpins the operations of businesses large and small.

1.2 Defining Cloud Computing

Cloud computing is a term that has become ubiquitous in the technology industry, but what exactly does it mean? At its core, cloud computing represents a fundamental shift in the way we think about and utilize computing resources. It's not just a buzzword; it's a transformative concept that has reshaped the IT landscape.

The NIST Definition

The National Institute of Standards and Technology (NIST) provides a widely accepted definition of cloud computing. According to NIST, cloud computing is defined as follows:

"Cloud computing is a model for enabling ubiquitous, convenient, on-demand network access to a shared pool of configurable computing resources (e.g., networks, servers, storage, applications, and services) that can be rapidly provisioned and released with minimal management effort or service provider interaction."

Let's break down this definition:

- **Ubiquitous Access:** Cloud computing allows users to access computing resources from anywhere with an internet connection. Whether you're at home, in the office, or on the go, the cloud is always within reach.
- **Convenient and On-Demand:** Cloud resources are available when you need them. You can provision and release resources on the fly, which means you no longer need to plan extensive hardware acquisitions and deployments.
- **Shared Pool:** The cloud operates as a shared environment where resources are pooled together and allocated dynamically. This sharing enables cost efficiency and resource optimization.
- **Configurable:** Cloud resources can be tailored to suit your specific needs. You can adjust computing power, storage capacity, and other resources as your requirements change.

- **Minimal Management Effort:** With cloud computing, much of the underlying infrastructure management is handled by the cloud provider. This reduces the burden on users and allows them to focus on their applications and data.
- **Service Provider Interaction:** Cloud services are typically delivered by third-party providers who manage the infrastructure. Users interact with these providers to access and manage their resources.

The Three Service Models

Cloud computing offers a variety of service models, each catering to different needs. The three primary service models are:

1. **Infrastructure as a Service (IaaS):** In an IaaS model, users are provided with virtualized computing resources, such as virtual machines, storage, and networking. This gives users the flexibility to create and manage their own infrastructure while offloading the underlying hardware management to the cloud provider.
2. **Platform as a Service (PaaS):** PaaS builds upon IaaS by offering a platform for developers to build, deploy, and manage applications without worrying about the underlying infrastructure. It includes tools and services for development, databases, and application hosting.
3. **Software as a Service (SaaS):** SaaS delivers software applications over the internet on a subscription basis. Users access these applications through web browsers, eliminating the need for local installations. Common examples include email services like Gmail and productivity suites like Microsoft Office 365.

1.3 Cloud Service Models (IaaS, PaaS, SaaS)

Cloud computing is not a one-size-fits-all concept. It offers a range of service models, each designed to meet specific needs and requirements. Understanding these service models is crucial as they define how users interact with and utilize cloud resources. The three primary service models are Infrastructure as a Service (IaaS), Platform as a Service (PaaS), and Software as a Service (SaaS).

1. *Infrastructure as a Service (IaaS): Building Blocks of the Cloud*

IaaS is the foundational layer of cloud computing. It provides users with virtualized computing resources over the internet. Think of IaaS as a blank canvas on which you can build your own infrastructure. Key characteristics of IaaS include:

- **Virtual Machines (VMs):** Users can create and manage virtual machines on which they can install and run their own operating systems and applications.
- **Storage:** IaaS providers offer scalable storage solutions, allowing users to store data in the cloud. It's flexible, cost-effective, and eliminates the need to manage physical storage devices.
- **Networking:** Users can configure and manage virtual networks, including firewalls, load balancers, and IP addresses.

IaaS is an ideal choice for users who want more control over their computing environment while benefiting from the scalability and cost-efficiency of the cloud. It's often used by businesses to host applications, websites, and development and testing environments.

*2. *Platform as a Service (PaaS): Empowering Developers*

PaaS takes cloud computing to the next level by offering a platform for developing, deploying, and managing applications without the complexities of infrastructure management. Key characteristics of PaaS include:

- **Development Tools:** PaaS platforms provide a range of development tools, frameworks, and services to streamline the application development process.

- **Middleware:** Users can leverage pre-built middleware components for tasks like database management, messaging, and authentication.
- **Application Hosting:** PaaS hosts the applications, automatically handling scalability, load balancing, and underlying infrastructure.

PaaS is an excellent choice for developers who want to focus on writing code rather than managing infrastructure. It accelerates development cycles, reduces operational overhead, and encourages innovation.

*3. *Software as a Service (SaaS): Ready-to-Use Applications

At the top of the cloud service model stack is SaaS. SaaS delivers fully functional software applications over the internet, accessible via web browsers. Key characteristics of SaaS include:

- **Ready-to-Use:** Users can access and use software applications without the need for installation or maintenance.
- **Subscription-Based:** SaaS is typically offered on a subscription basis, reducing upfront costs and providing ongoing updates and support.
- **Multi-Tenant:** SaaS applications serve multiple customers from a shared infrastructure, ensuring cost efficiency and scalability.

SaaS is prevalent in both personal and business settings, with examples ranging from email services like Gmail and productivity suites like Microsoft Office 365 to customer relationship management (CRM) tools like Salesforce.

Each of these cloud service models caters to different user needs and preferences. Whether you require control over infrastructure (IaaS), a streamlined development process (PaaS), or access to ready-to-use applications (SaaS), cloud computing provides the flexibility to choose the model that aligns with your objectives.

1.4 Cloud Deployment Models (Public, Private, Hybrid)

When you embark on your cloud computing journey, it's essential to understand the various deployment models available. Deployment models dictate where your cloud resources are hosted and who manages them. They offer different levels of control, security, and customization to suit diverse business and individual needs. The three primary cloud deployment models are Public Cloud, Private Cloud, and Hybrid Cloud.

1. *Public Cloud: The Global Playground*

The public cloud is perhaps the most well-known and widely used deployment model. In this model, cloud resources are owned, operated, and maintained by a third-party cloud service provider. These providers, including industry giants like Amazon Web Services (AWS), Microsoft Azure, and Google Cloud Platform (GCP), offer a range of services to users around the world. Key characteristics of the public cloud include:

- **Shared Infrastructure:** Resources in the public cloud are shared among multiple customers, resulting in cost efficiency and scalability.
- **Accessibility:** Users can access public cloud resources over the internet from anywhere with an internet connection.
- **Managed Services:** Public cloud providers handle infrastructure management, updates, and security, reducing the burden on users.

Public clouds are suitable for a wide range of use cases, from hosting websites and applications to data storage and processing. They are an excellent choice for businesses and individuals looking for flexibility and scalability without the upfront capital expenses.

2. *Private Cloud: Your Exclusive Domain*

Private clouds, as the name suggests, are dedicated cloud environments designed for a single organization. In this model, the organization retains complete control over the cloud infrastructure, which can be hosted on-premises or by a third-party provider. Key characteristics of private clouds include:

- **Isolation:** Private clouds offer isolation from other organizations, ensuring data security and compliance with regulatory requirements.
- **Customization:** Organizations can tailor the private cloud environment to their specific needs, including hardware, software, and security configurations.
- **Control:** IT teams have full control over the private cloud's infrastructure, allowing for precise management and customization.

Private clouds are often chosen by organizations with strict security and compliance needs, such as government agencies, financial institutions, and healthcare providers. They provide a high degree of control and customization while maintaining the benefits of cloud technology.

3. *Hybrid Cloud: Bridging Worlds*

The hybrid cloud model combines elements of both public and private clouds. It allows data and applications to move seamlessly between these environments, creating a flexible and dynamic computing environment. Key characteristics of hybrid clouds include:

- **Interoperability:** Hybrid clouds enable workloads to run in the most suitable environment, whether it's the public cloud for scalability or the private cloud for sensitive data.
- **Resource Flexibility:** Organizations can optimize resource allocation by using public cloud resources for peak workloads and private clouds for critical data.
- **Data Mobility:** Data can be shared and synchronized between public and private cloud environments as needed.

Hybrid clouds are a strategic choice for organizations seeking to balance control and scalability. They provide the flexibility to leverage the strengths of both public and private clouds while meeting changing business requirements.

1.5 Benefits of Cloud Computing

Cloud computing isn't just a technological advancement; it's a game-changer that has transformed the way we live, work, and do business. Its adoption has skyrocketed because of the numerous benefits it offers to individuals, organizations, and society as a whole.

1. Scalability and Flexibility: Grow with Ease

One of the most significant advantages of cloud computing is its scalability. In a traditional computing environment, scaling up your infrastructure to meet increased demand often involves significant costs and lead times. With the cloud, you can scale resources up or down on demand. Whether you're a startup experiencing rapid growth or an enterprise handling seasonal spikes in demand, the cloud accommodates your needs seamlessly.

2. Cost Efficiency: Pay as You Go

The pay-as-you-go model is a hallmark of cloud computing. Instead of investing in expensive hardware and software upfront, cloud users pay only for the resources they consume. This eliminates the need for substantial capital expenditures and allows businesses to allocate their budgets more efficiently. It's like paying for utilities—use more, pay more; use less, pay less.

3. Accessibility and Remote Work: Work from Anywhere

Cloud computing empowers remote work and remote access to data and applications. As long as you have an internet connection, you can access your work resources from virtually anywhere in the world.

This flexibility has become particularly crucial in today's world, where remote and hybrid work models have become the norm.

4. *Disaster Recovery and Data Security: Protect Your Assets*

Cloud providers invest heavily in data security and disaster recovery measures. Your data is stored in highly secure data centers with redundant backups, reducing the risk of data loss due to hardware failures or disasters. Many cloud providers offer robust security features and compliance certifications to ensure data protection.

5. *Automatic Updates and Maintenance: Stay Current with Ease*

Gone are the days of manual software updates and maintenance. Cloud providers handle these tasks automatically, ensuring that you always have access to the latest features and security patches. This reduces the burden on IT teams and minimizes downtime.

6. *Global Reach: Expand Your Horizons*

Cloud computing offers a global reach that was previously unimaginable. It allows businesses of all sizes to reach a worldwide customer base without the need for physical infrastructure in every location. This global presence enhances competitiveness and market reach.

7. *Environmental Impact: Reduce Your Carbon Footprint*

Cloud providers are making significant strides in sustainability. By consolidating data centers, optimizing energy usage, and investing in renewable energy sources, they help reduce the environmental impact of computing. Cloud adoption can lead to lower energy consumption and a smaller carbon footprint.

8. *Innovation and Agility: Stay Ahead of the Curve*

Cloud computing fosters innovation by providing access to cutting-edge technologies and services. It allows organizations to experiment, prototype, and deploy new applications rapidly. The agility it offers helps businesses respond quickly to changing market conditions and customer demands.

9. Cost Predictability: Budget with Confidence

With cloud computing, you can predict and control costs more effectively. The pay-as-you-go model, combined with transparent pricing, allows for accurate budgeting. There are no surprises or unexpected expenses.

These benefits of cloud computing have made it an indispensable tool for businesses and individuals alike. Whether you're looking to streamline your operations, reduce costs, improve accessibility, or drive innovation, the cloud can be a powerful ally in achieving your goals.

1.6 Challenges and Concerns

1. Security and Privacy: Protecting Your Data

Security is often the primary concern when it comes to cloud computing. Entrusting your data and applications to a third-party provider raises questions about data security and privacy. While cloud providers invest heavily in security measures, it's essential for users to understand their responsibilities regarding data protection. Proper encryption, access controls, and security policies are crucial to mitigate these risks.

2. Compliance and Regulations: Navigating the Legal Landscape

Different industries and regions have specific compliance requirements and regulations governing data handling and storage. When adopting cloud services, organizations must ensure that they comply with these laws. Navigating the complex landscape of compliance can be challenging, particularly for businesses with a global presence.

3. *Downtime and Service Outages: Managing Availability*

While cloud providers strive for high availability, service outages can still occur. These outages can disrupt business operations and impact productivity. It's essential for organizations to have contingency plans and consider the implications of potential downtime when using cloud services.

4. *Data Transfer and Bandwidth Costs: Managing Expenses*

Transferring data to and from the cloud can incur additional costs, particularly if you have large datasets. Organizations need to carefully monitor and manage their data transfer expenses to avoid unexpected charges.

5. *Vendor Lock-In: Ensuring Portability*

Vendor lock-in is a concern when an organization becomes heavily reliant on a particular cloud provider's services. Transitioning away from that provider can be complex and costly. To mitigate this risk, organizations can adopt multi-cloud or hybrid cloud strategies to maintain flexibility and portability.

6. *Lack of Control: Balancing Autonomy and Outsourcing*

Cloud computing involves relinquishing some control over infrastructure and services to third-party providers. While this can lead to cost savings and efficiency, it can also make organizations feel less in control of their IT environments. Finding the right balance between autonomy and outsourcing is a crucial consideration.

7. *Data Residency and Jurisdiction: Understanding Data Location*

Knowing where your data is stored and which jurisdiction it falls under is essential, especially for organizations with sensitive data or regulatory requirements. Some cloud providers offer data center locations in multiple regions, allowing users to choose where their data resides.

8. Cost Management: Avoiding Overspending

While cloud computing can be cost-effective, it's easy to overspend if resources are not managed efficiently. Without proper monitoring and cost management strategies, organizations can find themselves facing unexpectedly high bills.

9. Technical Challenges: Integration and Skills

Integrating existing on-premises systems with cloud services can be technically challenging. It requires expertise in cloud architecture and the ability to design and implement solutions that work seamlessly across hybrid environments. Additionally, organizations may need to invest in training and skills development to maximize the benefits of cloud technology.

It's important to note that these challenges are not insurmountable. With careful planning, diligent management, and a clear understanding of your organization's specific needs and goals, you can address these concerns and harness the full potential of cloud computing.

2: CLOUD INFRASTRUCTURE

2.1 Data Centers and Servers

2.1.1 Data Centers: The Fortresses of the Cloud

Imagine colossal structures housing countless racks of servers, sophisticated cooling systems, and redundant power supplies. These are data centers, the nerve centers of the cloud. Data centers are sprawling facilities designed to store and manage vast quantities of data and computing equipment. They come in various sizes, from small facilities serving local needs to massive data centers spread across multiple geographical locations to ensure redundancy and availability.

Key characteristics of data centers include:

- **Redundancy:** Data centers are built with redundancy in mind to ensure high availability. They have backup power sources, multiple network connections, and failover systems to minimize downtime.
- **Security:** Physical security is paramount. Access to data centers is tightly controlled, with biometric authentication, surveillance cameras, and security personnel ensuring that only authorized individuals gain entry.

- **Cooling and Environment:** Data centers generate significant heat, so cooling systems are critical to maintain optimal operating conditions. Temperature, humidity, and airflow are carefully managed to protect the equipment.
- **Scalability:** As the demand for cloud services grows, data centers must scale to accommodate more servers and storage devices. Cloud providers frequently expand their data center capacity to meet this demand.
- **Geographical Distribution:** Large cloud providers often have data centers in multiple locations around the world. This distribution improves performance, reduces latency, and provides geographic redundancy.

2.1.2 Servers: The Engines of Computation

Inside these data centers, you'll find servers—powerful computing machines that execute the tasks and processes that make cloud services possible. Servers come in various forms, but they all share the common goal of processing and delivering data to users and applications.

Key characteristics of servers include:

- **Processor (CPU):** The CPU is the brain of the server, responsible for executing instructions and computations. Modern servers often have multiple CPUs to handle parallel tasks.
- **Memory (RAM):** RAM provides fast, temporary storage for data and instructions that the CPU is actively using. More RAM allows servers to handle larger workloads.
- **Storage:** Servers have various types of storage, including hard disk drives (HDDs) and solid-state drives (SSDs). These store data and software that the server needs to operate.
- **Networking:** Servers are equipped with network interfaces to communicate with other servers, devices, and users. High-speed connections are crucial for efficient data transfer.
- **Operating System (OS):** Servers run specialized operating systems designed for stability, security, and performance.

Common server OS choices include Linux, Windows Server, and UNIX variants.

- **Virtualization:** Many servers in data centers are virtualized, meaning they can run multiple virtual machines (VMs) simultaneously. Virtualization maximizes resource utilization and flexibility.

Servers are often organized into clusters or racks within data centers, with each server optimized for specific tasks. These tasks can range from hosting websites and running databases to executing complex calculations for scientific research or artificial intelligence.

2.2 Virtualization

Virtualization allows multiple virtual instances of operating systems, applications, and data to run on a single physical server or across a cluster of servers. In essence, it creates an illusion of limitless computing resources by efficiently utilizing the available hardware.

2.2.1 How Virtualization Works

At the heart of virtualization is a piece of software known as a hypervisor or Virtual Machine Monitor (VMM). This hypervisor sits between the physical hardware (servers) and the virtual machines (VMs) and manages their interaction.

Here's how virtualization works:

- **Hypervisor:** The hypervisor abstracts and partitions the physical hardware into multiple virtual environments. Each of these virtual environments is a separate VM, complete with its own operating system (guest OS), applications, and resources.
- **Isolation:** VMs are isolated from one another, meaning that one VM cannot interfere with or access the resources of another. This isolation enhances security and stability.

- **Resource Allocation:** The hypervisor allocates CPU, memory, storage, and network resources to each VM based on predefined configurations or dynamic demand. This ensures that each VM gets the resources it needs to operate optimally.
- **Flexibility:** VMs can be created, moved, or deleted dynamically, allowing for rapid scalability and resource optimization. This flexibility is one of the key benefits of virtualization.

2.2.2 Types of Virtualization

Several types of virtualization techniques are employed in cloud environments. Here are some of the most common:

- **Server Virtualization:** This is the most fundamental form of virtualization, where a single physical server is divided into multiple VMs. It's the foundation of cloud computing and allows for efficient resource utilization.
- **Storage Virtualization:** Storage virtualization abstracts physical storage resources and presents them as a unified pool of storage, making it easier to manage and allocate storage capacity.
- **Network Virtualization:** Network virtualization creates virtual networks within a physical network infrastructure, enabling isolation, segmentation, and efficient use of network resources.
- **Desktop Virtualization:** Desktop virtualization, also known as Virtual Desktop Infrastructure (VDI), allows multiple virtual desktops to run on a single physical machine. It's commonly used in remote work scenarios and for centralized desktop management.
- **Application Virtualization:** Application virtualization separates an application from the underlying operating system, allowing it to run in a self-contained environment. This simplifies application management and compatibility.

2.2.3 Benefits of Virtualization

Virtualization brings a multitude of benefits to both cloud providers and users:

- **Resource Optimization:** By running multiple VMs on a single physical server, virtualization maximizes resource utilization, reducing hardware costs and energy consumption.
- **Flexibility and Scalability:** Virtualization allows for easy scaling of resources up or down based on demand. This agility is vital for cloud providers and businesses with fluctuating workloads.
- **Isolation and Security:** VM isolation enhances security by preventing one VM from accessing or affecting others. Security policies can be applied at the VM level.
- **Disaster Recovery:** Virtualization simplifies disaster recovery solutions by enabling the quick backup, replication, and restoration of VMs.
- **Testing and Development:** Developers can create and test applications in virtual environments that mirror production, reducing development time and errors.

2.3 Networking in the Cloud

2.3.1 The Importance of Networking

Networks are the backbone of cloud computing. They enable data to move between servers, storage devices, virtual machines, and ultimately, to the end-users or applications that rely on it. Networking in the cloud serves several essential functions:

- **Data Transfer:** Networks facilitate the transfer of data between different parts of the cloud infrastructure. This includes transmitting data from storage to computing resources, between virtual machines, and to end-users accessing cloud services.
- **Communication:** Networks enable communication between various cloud components, allowing them to work together

seamlessly. This includes interactions between servers, databases, and application services.

- **Accessibility:** Networks provide access to cloud services and resources from anywhere in the world, making it possible for users to connect to the cloud over the internet.
- **Security:** Networking plays a crucial role in ensuring the security of data in transit. Encryption and other security measures are used to protect data as it travels over networks.
- **Scalability:** Scalable networks allow cloud providers to handle increased traffic and demand. As more users and devices connect to the cloud, networks can adapt and expand to accommodate them.

2.3.2 Components of Cloud Networking

Cloud networking involves several key components and concepts:

- **Routers and Switches:** These devices form the foundation of network infrastructure, routing data packets to their destinations and managing network traffic.
- **Load Balancers:** Load balancers distribute incoming network traffic across multiple servers or resources to ensure optimal performance and redundancy.
- **Firewalls:** Firewalls are critical for network security, controlling incoming and outgoing traffic based on predefined security rules.
- **IP Addresses:** IP (Internet Protocol) addresses are unique identifiers assigned to each device on a network, allowing data packets to be directed to their intended destinations.
- **Subnets and VLANs:** Subnets and Virtual LANs (VLANs) help organize and segment networks for improved security and performance.
- **Content Delivery Networks (CDNs):** CDNs are networks of servers distributed globally to deliver content, such as web pages and multimedia, quickly and efficiently to end-users.
- **Software-Defined Networking (SDN):** SDN is an approach to networking that uses software-based controllers to manage and optimize network resources dynamically.

2.3.3 Cloud Networking Challenges

While cloud networking offers many advantages, it also presents challenges:

- **Latency:** Network latency, or delay, can impact the responsiveness of cloud applications. Minimizing latency is crucial for real-time applications like video conferencing and online gaming.
- **Bandwidth:** Ensuring sufficient network bandwidth to handle data traffic is essential. Inadequate bandwidth can lead to slow data transfer and reduced performance.
- **Security:** Securing cloud networks is a continuous challenge, with the constant threat of cyberattacks and data breaches.
- **Scalability:** As cloud usage grows, networks must scale to accommodate increased traffic and demand.
- **Interoperability:** Integrating on-premises networks with cloud networks and ensuring seamless communication can be complex.

Cloud providers invest heavily in network infrastructure and security to address these challenges and ensure reliable, high-performance network services.

2.4 Storage Solutions

2.4.1 The Role of Cloud Storage

Cloud storage is the backbone of data management in the cloud. It serves as the digital warehouse where organizations, individuals, and applications store, manage, and retrieve their data. Whether it's personal photos and documents, business records, or the databases that power applications, cloud storage solutions offer a versatile platform for data storage and access.

Key functions of cloud storage include:

- **Data Persistence:** Cloud storage ensures that data remains available even when devices are offline or replaced. It provides a central location for data that can be accessed from anywhere with an internet connection.
- **Scalability:** Cloud storage solutions can seamlessly scale to accommodate growing data volumes. As your data needs expand, additional storage capacity can be provisioned on-demand.
- **Redundancy:** Data is often replicated across multiple storage devices and data centers to ensure redundancy and protect against data loss due to hardware failures or disasters.
- **Accessibility:** Cloud storage solutions provide access controls and permissions, allowing users to manage who can access and modify data. This ensures data security and compliance.
- **Data Backup and Recovery:** Cloud storage services often include built-in backup and recovery features, making it easier to protect and restore data.

2.4.2 Types of Cloud Storage

Several types of cloud storage solutions cater to different use cases and data requirements:

- **Object Storage:** Object storage is ideal for unstructured data like images, videos, and documents. It stores data as objects, each with a unique identifier and metadata. Popular object storage services include Amazon S3 and Google Cloud Storage.
- **File Storage:** File storage is designed for managing structured data in a hierarchical file structure. It's similar to traditional file systems and is suitable for documents, media files, and shared data. Examples include Amazon EFS and Azure Files.
- **Block Storage:** Block storage provides raw storage volumes that can be attached to virtual machines and used as hard drives. It's commonly used for databases and applications that require low-level access to data. Services like Amazon EBS and Google Persistent Disks fall into this category.

- **Archival Storage:** Archival storage is cost-effective, long-term storage designed for infrequently accessed data. It's well-suited for compliance and data retention purposes. Amazon Glacier and Azure Archive Storage are examples.

2.4.3 Benefits of Cloud Storage

Cloud storage solutions offer a wide range of benefits:

- **Cost-Efficiency:** Pay-as-you-go pricing means you only pay for the storage you use, reducing upfront costs and providing predictable expenses.
- **Scalability:** Easily scale storage capacity up or down to meet changing needs without the need for hardware investments.
- **Redundancy and Durability:** Data is often stored redundantly in multiple data centers, ensuring high availability and durability.
- **Accessibility:** Access data from anywhere with an internet connection, fostering remote work and collaboration.
- **Security:** Cloud providers invest heavily in data security measures, including encryption and access controls.
- **Data Backup and Recovery:** Many cloud storage services offer automated backup and recovery options to protect against data loss.

2.5 Scalability and Elasticity

2.5.1 Scalability: Meeting Growing Needs

Scalability is the ability to expand or shrink resources in response to changes in demand. In the world of cloud computing, scalability is often categorized into two types:

- **Vertical Scalability (Scaling Up):** This involves increasing the capacity of a single resource. For example, adding more CPU, memory, or storage to a virtual machine to handle increased workloads.

- **Horizontal Scalability (Scaling Out):** Horizontal scalability involves adding more identical resources to a system. This could mean deploying additional virtual machines or servers to distribute the workload.

Cloud providers excel in delivering both vertical and horizontal scalability. Here's how it works:

- **Vertical Scalability:** Cloud users can resize their virtual machines (VMs) by allocating more CPU, memory, or storage resources as needed. This is often done with a few clicks or commands, making it quick and easy to accommodate increased demand.
- **Horizontal Scalability:** Cloud providers offer services like auto-scaling, which automatically adds or removes VM instances based on predefined rules or metrics. For instance, an e-commerce website might scale out to handle increased traffic during a holiday sale and scale back in during quieter periods.

Scalability ensures that businesses can grow seamlessly without significant capital investments in infrastructure. It also means they can handle sudden surges in demand without downtime or performance issues.

2.5.2 Elasticity: Dynamic Resource Allocation

Elasticity takes scalability to the next level by making resource allocation dynamic and automatic. In an elastic cloud environment, resources are provisioned and deprovisioned automatically based on real-time demand. Here's how it works:

- **Resource Provisioning:** When demand increases, the cloud system automatically provisions additional resources, such as virtual machines, storage, or network capacity.
- **Resource Deprovisioning:** Conversely, when demand decreases, the system deallocates or shuts down unnecessary resources to save costs.

Elasticity is particularly beneficial for applications and services with variable workloads, as it ensures optimal resource utilization without manual intervention.

2.5.3 Benefits of Scalability and Elasticity

The advantages of scalability and elasticity in cloud computing are numerous:

- **Cost-Efficiency:** Organizations pay only for the resources they use, avoiding over-provisioning and reducing operational expenses.
- **High Availability:** Scalability and elasticity contribute to high availability by ensuring resources are available to handle increased traffic or system failures.
- **Performance Optimization:** These capabilities enhance system performance by allowing applications to access additional resources when needed.
- **Improved User Experience:** Elasticity ensures a consistent user experience, even during traffic spikes.
- **Resource Optimization:** Resources are used efficiently, reducing waste and environmental impact.
- **Business Agility:** Scalability and elasticity empower businesses to respond rapidly to changing market conditions and customer demands.

2.6 Availability and Redundancy

2.6.1 Availability: The Measure of Uptime

Availability is a measure of how often a system, service, or resource is operational and accessible. It's typically expressed as a percentage and refers to the amount of time a system is "up" and available for use.

For example, a cloud service with 99.9% availability is expected to be operational and accessible for 99.9% of the time in a given period, typically a year. This equates to about 8.76 hours of allowable downtime annually.

Cloud providers strive to offer high availability to ensure that their services are reliable and accessible. Achieving high availability involves various strategies and technologies, including:

- **Redundancy:** Deploying redundant hardware, data centers, and network connections to eliminate single points of failure.
- **Load Balancing:** Distributing incoming traffic across multiple servers or resources to prevent overloading and ensure responsiveness.
- **Failover:** Automatically switching to backup systems or resources in case of a failure to minimize downtime.
- **Geographic Distribution:** Placing data centers in multiple regions to enhance availability and disaster recovery.
- **Continuous Monitoring:** Proactively monitoring systems and services to detect and address issues before they impact users.

2.6.2 Redundancy: The Safety Net

Redundancy is the practice of duplicating critical components, systems, or data to ensure that there is a backup available in case of failure. It's a fundamental concept in cloud computing and plays a pivotal role in achieving high availability.

Here are some common forms of redundancy in the cloud:

- **Data Redundancy:** Data is often replicated across multiple storage devices or data centers. This redundancy safeguards against data loss due to hardware failures or disasters.
- **Server Redundancy:** Cloud providers use redundant servers to ensure that applications and services remain accessible even if one server fails. Load balancers distribute traffic among these servers.
- **Network Redundancy:** Multiple network connections and paths are established to prevent network outages. If one

connection fails, traffic is automatically rerouted through an alternate path.

- **Geographic Redundancy:** Cloud providers often have data centers in different geographical locations. This geographic diversity enhances redundancy and disaster recovery capabilities.
- **Power Redundancy:** Backup power supplies, such as uninterruptible power supplies (UPS) and generators, ensure that data centers continue to operate during power outages.
- **Hardware Redundancy:** Critical hardware components, such as CPUs and memory, may be duplicated within servers to prevent hardware failures from causing service interruptions.

2.6.3 Benefits of Availability and Redundancy

The benefits of availability and redundancy in cloud computing are evident:

- **Reliability:** High availability ensures that cloud services are reliable, and users can access them when needed.
- **Continuous Operations:** Redundancy minimizes downtime, ensuring that services remain operational even in the face of hardware failures or other issues.
- **Disaster Recovery:** Geographic redundancy and data replication enhance disaster recovery capabilities, reducing data loss and downtime in the event of a catastrophe.
- **Improved User Experience:** A highly available and redundant system provides a seamless user experience, fostering trust and satisfaction.
- **Business Continuity:** Availability and redundancy strategies contribute to business continuity by ensuring that critical operations can continue in adverse conditions.

3: CLOUD SERVICES

3.1 Infrastructure as a Service (IaaS)

3.1.1 What is IaaS?

Infrastructure as a Service, or IaaS, is one of the fundamental categories of cloud services. It provides users with on-demand access to virtualized computing resources hosted in the cloud. These resources include:

- **Virtual Machines (VMs):** IaaS allows you to create and manage virtual machines, which are essentially software-based representations of physical servers. You can choose the operating system, install software, and configure the VM to meet your specific needs.
- **Storage:** IaaS offers scalable and flexible storage solutions, allowing you to store data, files, and backups in the cloud. Storage can be easily expanded as your requirements grow.
- **Networking:** With IaaS, you can set up and manage networking components like virtual private networks (VPNs), firewalls, and load balancers. This enables you to create secure and customized network environments.
- **Operating Systems:** IaaS providers often offer a variety of pre-configured operating system images, making it easy to launch virtual machines with your choice of OS.

IaaS is all about flexibility and control. It empowers users to design and manage their virtual infrastructure without the need for physical hardware. This means you can scale your resources up or down as needed, experiment with new configurations, and maintain control over your environment.

3.1.2 Benefits of IaaS

IaaS brings a range of benefits to the table, making it a popular choice for businesses and individuals:

- **Scalability:** IaaS allows you to scale your infrastructure to meet changing demands. If your website experiences a traffic surge or your application requires more processing power, you can quickly provision additional resources.
- **Cost-Efficiency:** By eliminating the need to invest in and maintain physical hardware, IaaS reduces capital expenses. You pay only for the resources you use, making it a cost-effective solution.
- **Speed and Agility:** With IaaS, you can rapidly deploy and configure virtual resources, reducing the time it takes to launch new services or applications.
- **Flexibility:** IaaS gives you the freedom to experiment with different configurations, test software, and adapt to evolving technology trends.
- **Disaster Recovery:** Cloud-based storage and backup solutions offered by IaaS providers enhance disaster recovery capabilities, ensuring data resilience.
- **Global Reach:** Many IaaS providers have data centers located worldwide, allowing you to deploy resources close to your target audience for improved performance and user experience.

3.1.3 Common IaaS Providers

Several prominent cloud providers offer IaaS solutions, each with its own set of features and services. Some of the well-known IaaS providers include:

- **Amazon Web Services (AWS):** AWS is one of the largest and most comprehensive IaaS providers, offering a vast array of services for computing, storage, and networking.
- **Microsoft Azure:** Azure provides a wide range of IaaS offerings, seamlessly integrating with Microsoft products and services.
- **Google Cloud Platform (GCP):** GCP offers IaaS solutions alongside its suite of cloud services, emphasizing data analytics and machine learning capabilities.
- **IBM Cloud:** IBM's cloud infrastructure is known for its focus on enterprise-grade solutions and hybrid cloud capabilities.
- **Oracle Cloud Infrastructure (OCI):** OCI provides IaaS solutions with a focus on database services and cloud security.

3.1.4 Use Cases for IaaS

IaaS is suitable for a variety of use cases, including:

- **Web Hosting:** Hosting websites and web applications in a scalable and cost-effective manner.
- **Development and Testing:** Creating development and testing environments with on-demand resources.
- **Data Backup and Recovery:** Storing and safeguarding data backups in the cloud for disaster recovery purposes.
- **Big Data and Analytics:** Processing and analyzing large datasets using scalable computing resources.
- **Hybrid Cloud:** Extending on-premises infrastructure into the cloud for increased flexibility and resource utilization.
- **Content Delivery:** Distributing media and content globally through content delivery networks (CDNs).

3.2 Platform as a Service (PaaS)

3.2.1 What is PaaS?

Platform as a Service (PaaS) is a category of cloud computing that provides a platform and environment for developers to build, deploy, and manage applications. PaaS abstracts the underlying infrastructure and handles many of the tasks associated with application development and deployment, including:

- **Server Management:** PaaS eliminates the need to manage physical or virtual servers. Developers can focus on coding, while the platform takes care of server provisioning, scaling, and maintenance.
- **Operating System:** The underlying operating system is managed by the PaaS provider, freeing developers from OS updates and configurations.
- **Development Tools:** PaaS platforms often include integrated development tools, frameworks, and libraries to streamline application development.
- **Database Management:** PaaS provides database services and automates database management tasks like backups, scaling, and maintenance.
- **Scaling:** PaaS platforms offer automatic scaling based on application demand, ensuring optimal performance during traffic spikes.

PaaS is particularly valuable for development teams because it accelerates the development process, reduces operational overhead, and allows developers to focus on writing code and building features rather than managing infrastructure.

3.2.2 Benefits of PaaS

PaaS offers a range of benefits that make it a popular choice for developers and organizations:

- **Speed and Efficiency:** PaaS accelerates application development by providing pre-configured environments and tools. Developers can write code and deploy applications more quickly.

- **Cost-Efficiency:** With PaaS, you only pay for the resources and services you use. This eliminates the need for capital investments in infrastructure.
- **Scalability:** PaaS platforms handle application scaling automatically, ensuring that your application can grow to meet user demand.
- **Simplified Maintenance:** PaaS providers take care of server maintenance, security updates, and operating system management, reducing the operational burden on development teams.
- **Collaboration:** PaaS platforms often include collaboration features that allow development teams to work together seamlessly, regardless of their physical locations.
- **Focus on Innovation:** By abstracting infrastructure management, PaaS allows developers to concentrate on innovation and building features that differentiate their applications.

3.2.3 Common PaaS Providers

Several cloud providers offer PaaS solutions, each with its own set of features and services. Some well-known PaaS providers include:

- **Heroku:** Heroku is a PaaS platform that simplifies application deployment and management. It supports multiple programming languages and offers a range of add-ons and extensions.
- **Google App Engine:** App Engine is Google's PaaS offering, designed for building and deploying web applications and APIs. It supports multiple languages and provides automatic scaling.
- **Microsoft Azure App Service:** Azure's PaaS platform provides a comprehensive environment for building, deploying, and scaling web and mobile applications. It supports various programming languages and integrates with other Azure services.
- **IBM Cloud Foundry:** IBM's PaaS solution, based on Cloud Foundry, offers a platform for building, deploying, and

managing applications. It provides a range of development tools and services.

- **Red Hat OpenShift:** OpenShift is a Kubernetes-based PaaS platform that offers developer-friendly tools for containerized application development and deployment.

3.2.4 Use Cases for PaaS

PaaS is well-suited for a variety of application development scenarios, including:

- **Web Application Development:** PaaS simplifies the development and deployment of web applications, making it an ideal choice for startups and web-focused businesses.
- **Mobile App Development:** PaaS platforms often provide tools and services for building and deploying mobile applications on various platforms.
- **API Development:** PaaS makes it easy to create, manage, and deploy APIs, allowing organizations to expose their services to external developers.
- **IoT Application Development:** Developing applications for the Internet of Things (IoT) can be streamlined with PaaS, as it handles the backend infrastructure required for IoT solutions.
- **Microservices and Containerized Applications:** PaaS platforms that support container orchestration, such as Kubernetes-based solutions, are well-suited for microservices and containerized application architectures.

3.3 Software as a Service (SaaS)

3.3.1 What is SaaS?

Software as a Service (SaaS) is a cloud computing model that provides access to software applications hosted and maintained by a third-party provider. Instead of installing and running software on local devices or servers, users can access the software through a web browser. SaaS eliminates the need for users to manage installation, maintenance, updates, and infrastructure.

Key characteristics of SaaS include:

- **Accessibility:** SaaS applications are accessible from anywhere with an internet connection, making them ideal for remote work and collaboration.
- **Subscription-Based:** SaaS is typically offered on a subscription basis, with users paying a recurring fee to use the software. This subscription model often includes updates, support, and maintenance.
- **Multi-Tenancy:** SaaS providers use a multi-tenant architecture, where a single instance of the software serves multiple customers. Each customer's data and configurations are kept separate and secure.
- **Automatic Updates:** SaaS providers handle software updates and patches, ensuring users always have access to the latest features and security enhancements.
- **Scalability:** SaaS applications can scale to accommodate growing user bases and changing demands.

SaaS has revolutionized the way businesses and individuals access and use software, offering an array of applications for various purposes, from productivity and collaboration tools to customer relationship management and data analytics.

3.3.2 Benefits of SaaS

SaaS offers numerous advantages that have made it a preferred choice for businesses and users alike:

- **Cost-Efficiency:** The subscription model eliminates the need for upfront software purchases and reduces total cost of ownership. Users pay only for what they use.
- **Accessibility:** SaaS applications are accessible from any device with internet access, enabling flexible work arrangements and remote access.

- **Automatic Updates:** Software updates and maintenance are handled by the provider, ensuring that users always have access to the latest features and security enhancements.
- **Collaboration:** SaaS tools often include collaboration features, making it easy for teams to work together on projects and documents in real time.
- **Scalability:** SaaS applications can scale up or down to accommodate changing user requirements, making them suitable for businesses of all sizes.
- **Reduced IT Overhead:** SaaS eliminates the need for in-house IT resources to manage software installations and updates.

3.3.3 Common SaaS Applications

SaaS spans a wide range of application categories, catering to various needs and industries. Some common types of SaaS applications include:

- **Productivity Suites:** Examples include Microsoft 365 (formerly Office 365) and Google Workspace, which provide tools for word processing, spreadsheets, email, and collaboration.
- **Customer Relationship Management (CRM):** Salesforce and HubSpot offer CRM solutions for managing customer interactions and relationships.
- **Human Resources (HR) and Talent Management:** SaaS HR software like Workday and BambooHR streamlines HR processes, including payroll, benefits, and recruitment.
- **Collaboration and Communication:** Tools like Slack and Zoom facilitate communication, video conferencing, and collaboration among teams.
- **Project Management:** Trello, Asana, and Jira are SaaS project management tools that help teams organize and track tasks and projects.
- **Accounting and Finance:** QuickBooks and Xero are SaaS accounting software solutions that assist with financial management and reporting.

- **E-commerce Platforms:** Shopify and BigCommerce provide SaaS e-commerce solutions for businesses looking to sell products online.

3.3.4 Use Cases for SaaS

SaaS is suitable for a wide range of use cases, including:

- **Office Productivity:** SaaS productivity suites offer tools for document creation, email, and collaboration, making them ideal for businesses of all sizes.
- **Customer Management:** SaaS CRM systems help businesses track customer interactions, manage leads, and improve customer relationships.
- **Communication and Collaboration:** SaaS communication tools enable remote work, video conferencing, and team collaboration.
- **Content Management:** SaaS content management systems (CMS) like WordPress and Drupal make it easy to create and manage websites and blogs.
- **Analytics and Business Intelligence:** SaaS analytics platforms allow businesses to analyze data and gain insights into their operations.
- **Marketing Automation:** SaaS marketing automation tools help businesses automate marketing campaigns, track customer engagement, and generate leads.
- **E-learning and Education:** SaaS e-learning platforms provide online education and training solutions for schools, universities, and businesses.

3.4 Function as a Service (FaaS)

3.4.1 What is FaaS?

Function as a Service (FaaS), also known as serverless computing, is a cloud computing model that allows developers to run individual functions or units of code in response to specific events or triggers.

In FaaS, developers write code in the form of functions, and the cloud provider takes care of the infrastructure required to execute those functions. Developers simply upload their code and specify the events or triggers that should activate it.

Key characteristics of FaaS include:

- **Event-Driven:** FaaS functions are typically triggered by events such as HTTP requests, database changes, file uploads, or timer-based intervals.
- **Automatic Scaling:** FaaS platforms automatically scale the execution environment to accommodate the workload, ensuring that functions can handle varying levels of traffic.
- **Billing Model:** FaaS platforms charge users based on the number of function executions and the duration of each execution, making it a cost-effective model.
- **Stateless:** FaaS functions are designed to be stateless, meaning they do not maintain any local state between invocations. State is often stored in external databases or services.
- **No Server Management:** Developers do not need to manage servers, operating systems, or infrastructure configurations. They focus solely on writing code.

FaaS is particularly well-suited for building applications with event-driven architectures, microservices, and highly scalable components.

3.4.2 Benefits of FaaS

Function as a Service (FaaS) offers several advantages that have contributed to its popularity among developers and organizations:

- **Cost-Efficiency:** FaaS platforms charge users based on actual usage, eliminating the need for continuous infrastructure provisioning and reducing operational costs.
- **Scalability:** FaaS platforms automatically scale functions to handle varying workloads, ensuring optimal performance without manual intervention.

- **Reduced Development Time:** Developers can focus on writing code rather than managing infrastructure, resulting in faster development cycles.
- **Flexibility:** FaaS supports a wide range of use cases, from simple automation tasks to complex, event-driven applications.
- **Event-Driven Architecture:** FaaS naturally aligns with event-driven architectures, making it suitable for real-time applications and services.
- **High Availability:** FaaS providers often offer built-in redundancy and high availability for functions.

3.4.3 Common FaaS Providers

Several cloud providers offer Function as a Service (FaaS) solutions, each with its own set of features and services. Some well-known FaaS providers include:

- **AWS Lambda:** Amazon Web Services (AWS) Lambda is a serverless computing service that allows developers to run code in response to events. It supports multiple programming languages and integrates with various AWS services.
- **Azure Functions:** Azure Functions is Microsoft's serverless offering, providing an event-driven platform for running code in response to triggers. It supports multiple programming languages and integrates with Azure services.
- **Google Cloud Functions:** Google Cloud Functions is a serverless compute service on Google Cloud Platform (GCP). It enables developers to write functions in Node.js, Python, or Go and trigger them in response to events.
- **IBM Cloud Functions:** IBM Cloud Functions is IBM's serverless platform that allows developers to build and deploy functions in response to events. It supports multiple programming languages and integrates with IBM Cloud services.
- **Alibaba Cloud Function Compute:** Alibaba Cloud Function Compute is a serverless compute service that enables developers to run functions in response to events. It

supports multiple programming languages and integrates with Alibaba Cloud services.

3.4.4 Use Cases for FaaS

Function as a Service (FaaS) is suitable for a variety of use cases, including:

- **Real-Time Data Processing:** FaaS functions can process real-time data streams, enabling applications like real-time analytics and monitoring.
- **API Backends:** FaaS is often used to create lightweight API endpoints for mobile applications and web services.
- **Automation and Workflows:** FaaS functions can automate repetitive tasks, such as data transformations, file processing, and database updates.
- **IoT Data Processing:** FaaS platforms can process data generated by Internet of Things (IoT) devices, allowing for real-time analysis and decision-making.
- **Image and Video Processing:** Functions can be used for image and video processing tasks, such as thumbnail generation, resizing, and object recognition.
- **Scheduled Tasks:** FaaS functions can be scheduled to run at specific times or intervals, making them suitable for tasks like data backups and report generation.

3.5 Other Cloud Services (Database as a Service, CDN, etc.)

Beyond the core categories of cloud services like IaaS, PaaS, SaaS, and FaaS, the cloud offers a vast array of specialized services that cater to specific needs and requirements.

3.5.1 Database as a Service (DBaaS)

Database as a Service (DBaaS) is a cloud computing model that provides database management and hosting as a service. With DBaaS, users can access and manage databases without the need to set up and maintain physical servers or database software. Some key features of DBaaS include:

- **Managed Databases:** DBaaS providers offer managed database instances, allowing users to focus on data and applications rather than database administration.
- **Scalability:** Users can easily scale database resources up or down to meet changing demands.
- **Security:** DBaaS providers implement security measures to protect data, including encryption, access controls, and backups.
- **Automated Backups:** DBaaS platforms often include automated backup and recovery options to safeguard data.
- **Multi-Platform Support:** DBaaS supports various database engines such as MySQL, PostgreSQL, MongoDB, and others.

DBaaS simplifies database management, making it accessible to businesses and developers without dedicated database expertise.

3.5.2 Content Delivery Networks (CDN)

Content Delivery Networks (CDN) are a network of distributed servers strategically positioned around the world to deliver web content and applications to users more efficiently. Key features of CDNs include:

- **Caching:** CDNs cache static content like images, scripts, and videos on their servers, reducing load times for users.
- **Global Distribution:** CDNs have servers in multiple geographic locations, enabling faster content delivery to users in different regions.
- **Distributed Denial of Service (DDoS) Protection:** CDNs offer DDoS mitigation services to protect websites and applications from attacks.
- **Load Balancing:** CDNs distribute incoming traffic across multiple servers to prevent overloads and improve reliability.

- **Secure Sockets Layer (SSL) Termination:** CDNs often provide SSL termination services to offload SSL processing from origin servers.

CDNs enhance the performance, security, and availability of websites and applications, making them an integral part of the modern internet landscape.

3.5.3 Internet of Things (IoT) Services

The **Internet of Things (IoT)** is a network of interconnected devices, sensors, and objects that collect and exchange data. Cloud providers offer specialized IoT services to facilitate IoT application development and management. These services include:

- **Device Management:** IoT platforms provide tools for managing IoT devices, including provisioning, configuration, and monitoring.
- **Data Ingestion and Analytics:** IoT services support data ingestion from devices and enable real-time data analysis for insights and decision-making.
- **Security:** IoT platforms include security features to protect data and devices from threats.
- **Scalability:** IoT services are designed to scale and accommodate a growing number of devices and data.

IoT services empower organizations to harness the potential of IoT by simplifying device management and data analysis.

3.5.4 Machine Learning and Artificial Intelligence (AI)

Cloud providers offer specialized services for **Machine Learning (ML)** and **Artificial Intelligence (AI)**, allowing businesses and developers to build and deploy ML and AI models. These services include:

- **ML Model Training:** Cloud platforms provide tools and infrastructure for training machine learning models using large datasets.

- **Predictive Analytics:** ML and AI services enable predictive analytics for applications like recommendation engines and fraud detection.
- **Natural Language Processing (NLP):** Cloud providers offer NLP services for processing and analyzing human language data.
- **Computer Vision:** AI services support computer vision applications, such as image and video analysis.
- **Speech Recognition:** Cloud platforms offer speech recognition capabilities for voice-controlled applications and virtual assistants.

ML and AI services bring advanced capabilities to applications, enabling them to learn from data and make intelligent decisions.

3.5.5 Blockchain Services

Blockchain is a distributed ledger technology that provides transparency, security, and immutability for transactions and data. Cloud providers offer **Blockchain as a Service (BaaS)** to simplify the deployment and management of blockchain networks. BaaS services typically include:

- **Network Provisioning:** BaaS platforms allow users to provision blockchain networks with predefined configurations.
- **Smart Contracts:** BaaS services support the development and deployment of smart contracts on blockchain networks.
- **Scalability:** BaaS platforms provide scalability options for blockchain networks as the number of participants and transactions grows.
- **Security:** BaaS platforms include security features to protect blockchain networks from attacks.

Blockchain services are ideal for businesses looking to harness the benefits of blockchain technology without the complexity of managing a blockchain network.

3.5.6 Identity and Access Management (IAM)

Identity and Access Management (IAM) services provide tools and capabilities for managing user identities, access controls, and authentication in the cloud. IAM services enable organizations to:

- **Manage User Identities:** Create, manage, and secure user accounts and access to cloud resources.
- **Access Controls:** Define and enforce access policies and permissions for users and resources.
- **Authentication:** Implement multi-factor authentication (MFA) and single sign-on (SSO) for added security.

IAM services are crucial for maintaining the security and compliance of cloud-based applications and resources.

4: CLOUD PROVIDERS

4.1 Major Cloud Providers (Amazon Web Services, Microsoft Azure, Google Cloud)

4.1.1 Amazon Web Services (AWS)

Amazon Web Services (AWS), launched in 2006, is often credited with pioneering the modern cloud computing era. With an extensive global network of data centers, AWS provides a vast array of cloud services across computing, storage, databases, machine learning, analytics, and more. Some key features of AWS include:

- **Global Reach:** AWS boasts a global presence with data centers in multiple regions and Availability Zones, allowing users to deploy resources close to their target audiences.
- **Service Portfolio:** AWS offers over 200 services, including Amazon EC2 for virtual computing, Amazon S3 for scalable storage, and Amazon RDS for managed databases.
- **Market Leadership:** AWS is the market leader in cloud services, trusted by startups, enterprises, and governments worldwide.
- **Security and Compliance:** AWS provides robust security features, compliance certifications, and identity and access management tools.

- **Ecosystem:** AWS has a rich ecosystem of partners, third-party tools, and a vibrant developer community.

4.1.2 Microsoft Azure

Microsoft Azure, introduced in 2010, is Microsoft's cloud platform that integrates seamlessly with the company's software products and services. Azure offers a comprehensive set of cloud solutions, including virtual machines, databases, AI and machine learning, and IoT. Key highlights of Azure include:

- **Hybrid Cloud Capability:** Azure enables businesses to seamlessly integrate on-premises data centers with the cloud, providing a hybrid cloud solution.
- **Enterprise Integration:** Azure offers strong integration with Microsoft products such as Windows Server, SQL Server, and Active Directory.
- **AI and Machine Learning:** Azure provides a suite of AI and machine learning tools, including Azure Machine Learning and Azure Cognitive Services.
- **Developer-Friendly:** Azure supports multiple programming languages, frameworks, and tools, making it developer-friendly.
- **Global Network:** Azure operates in regions across the globe, ensuring low-latency access to cloud resources.

4.1.3 Google Cloud

Google Cloud, launched in 2011, leverages Google's expertise in data centers, networking, and machine learning to offer cloud services. Google Cloud is known for its data analytics and machine learning capabilities, along with a strong emphasis on open source technologies. Key attributes of Google Cloud include:

- **Data Analytics:** Google Cloud provides BigQuery for data warehousing and data analytics at scale.
- **Machine Learning:** Google Cloud offers a suite of machine learning tools, including TensorFlow and AI Platform.

- **Global Network Backbone:** Google Cloud benefits from Google's extensive global network infrastructure, ensuring high-speed connectivity.
- **Open Source Commitment:** Google Cloud embraces open source technologies and contributes to open source projects.
- **Data and Analytics:** Google Cloud offers a wide range of data storage and analytics services, including Google Cloud Storage and Google Data Studio.

These major cloud providers have each carved out their unique niches and strengths in the cloud computing world. While AWS, Azure, and Google Cloud are the frontrunners, numerous other cloud providers offer specialized services and cater to specific industries and use cases.

4.2 Smaller Cloud Providers and Specialized Services

4.2.1 Smaller Cloud Providers

Smaller cloud providers, often referred to as "alternative" or "niche" providers, play a vital role in the cloud ecosystem. These providers may not match the scale and global reach of the major players, but they offer distinct advantages, such as personalized service, specialized expertise, and unique solutions. Here are a few notable smaller cloud providers:

- **IBM Cloud:** IBM Cloud offers a range of cloud services, including infrastructure, AI, and blockchain. It is known for its focus on hybrid and multicloud solutions.
- **Oracle Cloud:** Oracle Cloud provides cloud services geared toward enterprise applications, databases, and cloud-native development.
- **Alibaba Cloud:** Alibaba Cloud, a subsidiary of Alibaba Group, is a leading cloud provider in Asia and offers a wide array of cloud services with a strong presence in China.

- **DigitalOcean:** DigitalOcean specializes in providing simple and developer-friendly cloud infrastructure for startups and developers.
- **Rackspace Technology:** Rackspace offers managed cloud services and specializes in providing expertise in managing cloud environments.

These smaller cloud providers often differentiate themselves by targeting specific industries, offering unique services, and providing a more personalized approach to customer support.

4.2.2 Specialized Cloud Services

In addition to smaller cloud providers, the cloud ecosystem is enriched by specialized services that cater to specific use cases and industries. These services can be offered by both major and smaller providers. Let's explore a few categories of specialized cloud services:

- **Content Delivery Networks (CDN):** CDNs like Cloudflare and Akamai provide distributed content delivery, improving the performance and security of websites and applications.
- **Database as a Service (DBaaS):** DBaaS providers like MongoDB Atlas and Aiven offer managed database solutions, simplifying database administration.
- **Serverless Computing:** Serverless platforms like Netlify and Vercel focus on simplifying the deployment of serverless functions for web applications.
- **Managed Kubernetes Services:** Managed Kubernetes providers like DigitalOcean Kubernetes and Red Hat OpenShift simplify the deployment and management of containerized applications.
- **IoT Platforms:** IoT platforms like AWS IoT Core and Microsoft Azure IoT Hub offer specialized services for building and managing Internet of Things applications.
- **DevOps and Continuous Integration/Continuous Deployment (CI/CD):** Services like Travis CI and CircleCI specialize in automating the software development and deployment pipelines.

- **Blockchain Platforms:** Blockchain service providers like Chainstack and BaaSify offer solutions for building and managing blockchain networks.

These specialized services address specific technical challenges and requirements, making them invaluable for businesses and developers with niche needs.

4.2.3 Choosing the Right Cloud Provider

Selecting the right cloud provider is a critical decision for businesses and individuals. The choice should align with your specific needs, budget, and technical requirements. When evaluating cloud providers, consider the following factors:

- **Service Offerings:** Assess the range of services offered by the provider, including compute, storage, databases, and specialized services relevant to your use case.
- **Pricing and Cost Structure:** Understand the provider's pricing model, including subscription plans, pay-as-you-go options, and potential cost savings.
- **Compliance and Security:** Evaluate the provider's security measures, compliance certifications, and data protection capabilities, especially if you have regulatory requirements.
- **Ecosystem and Integration:** Consider the provider's ecosystem of partners, third-party integrations, and developer tools.
- **Global Reach:** Assess the provider's global network infrastructure, data center locations, and the ability to serve your target regions.
- **Customer Support:** Review the provider's customer support options, including documentation, community forums, and premium support services.
- **Scalability and Performance:** Ensure that the provider can meet your scalability and performance requirements as your workload grows.
- **Vendor Lock-In:** Consider the potential for vendor lock-in and whether the provider offers tools for data migration and interoperability.

4.3 Comparing Cloud Providers

Selecting the right cloud provider is a critical decision for any organization or individual venturing into the cloud. Each cloud provider brings its unique strengths, services, and pricing models to the table. To make an informed choice, it's essential to evaluate and compare cloud providers based on specific criteria that align with your needs and goals.

4.3.1 Service Offerings

The first and most fundamental aspect to assess is the range of services offered by a cloud provider. Consider the following:

- **Compute Services:** Evaluate the types of virtual machines (VMs) and compute resources available. Does the provider offer a variety of VM sizes to accommodate different workloads?
- **Storage Services:** Examine the storage options, including object storage, block storage, and file storage. Assess the scalability and durability of storage solutions.
- **Database Services:** Look at the managed database offerings. Does the provider support a wide range of database engines like MySQL, PostgreSQL, NoSQL, etc.?
- **Networking:** Review the networking capabilities, including virtual networks, load balancers, and content delivery networks (CDNs).
- **Specialized Services:** Investigate whether the provider offers specialized services like machine learning, IoT, DevOps, and analytics.
- **Developer Tools:** Assess the availability of developer tools, SDKs, and integrated development environments (IDEs).

4.3.2 Pricing and Cost Structure

Cloud pricing can be complex, with multiple factors influencing costs. It's crucial to understand the provider's pricing model and cost structure:

- **Pricing Plans:** Examine the pricing plans offered, such as pay-as-you-go, reserved instances, or subscription models.
- **Pricing Transparency:** Ensure that the provider offers clear and transparent pricing information, including calculator tools to estimate costs.
- **Cost Management:** Evaluate the availability of cost management and monitoring tools to help track and optimize expenses.
- **Potential Discounts:** Check if the provider offers discounts for long-term commitments or usage commitments.
- **Free Tier:** Look for a free tier or trial period that allows you to test the services before committing to paid plans.

4.3.3 Security and Compliance

Security and compliance are paramount when choosing a cloud provider:

- **Security Features:** Assess the provider's security features, including encryption, firewall capabilities, identity and access management (IAM), and security monitoring.
- **Compliance Certifications:** Determine whether the provider complies with industry-specific certifications and regulatory requirements relevant to your organization.
- **Data Protection:** Investigate data protection measures, backup and disaster recovery options, and data residency options.
- **Incident Response:** Review the provider's incident response and recovery procedures in case of security breaches or service interruptions.

4.3.4 Ecosystem and Integration

The provider's ecosystem can greatly impact your ability to integrate with other tools and services:

- **Partners and Marketplace:** Explore the provider's ecosystem of partners and third-party integrations. A robust ecosystem can offer a wide range of additional services.
- **Developer Support:** Look for a vibrant developer community, documentation, and support resources to assist with integration and development.
- **Interoperability:** Consider whether the provider offers tools and services for interoperability with other cloud providers or on-premises infrastructure.

4.3.5 Global Reach

If your organization operates internationally, the global reach of the cloud provider is a crucial consideration:

- **Data Center Locations:** Assess the provider's data center locations and the ability to deploy resources in regions that align with your target audience.
- **Content Delivery:** Examine the availability of content delivery networks (CDNs) to ensure fast and reliable content delivery worldwide.

4.3.6 Customer Support

Finally, evaluate the customer support options provided by the cloud provider:

- **Documentation:** Review the quality and comprehensiveness of the provider's documentation and knowledge base.
- **Support Tiers:** Determine the availability of support tiers, including standard, premium, and enterprise support options.
- **Response Times:** Understand the provider's response times for support requests and the availability of 24/7 support.
- **Community Resources:** Consider the availability of user forums, community-driven support, and developer communities.

4.4 How to Choose the Right Cloud Provider

Choosing the right cloud provider is a significant decision that can impact your organization's success in the cloud. To make an informed choice, you need a structured approach that takes into account your specific needs, goals, and constraints.

4.4.1 Define Your Requirements

The first step in choosing a cloud provider is to clearly define your requirements. Consider the following questions:

- **What Are Your Goals?** Determine your primary objectives for moving to the cloud. Are you looking to reduce costs, increase scalability, improve agility, or enhance security?
- **What Workloads Will You Run?** Identify the types of workloads you plan to run in the cloud, such as web applications, databases, analytics, or machine learning.
- **Geographic Scope:** Determine the geographic regions where you need cloud resources. Some providers have a stronger presence in specific regions.
- **Technical Requirements:** Assess your technical requirements, including operating systems, programming languages, and integration with existing tools and services.
- **Compliance Needs:** Identify any regulatory or compliance requirements that apply to your industry or organization.

4.4.2 Evaluate Service Offerings

Once you've defined your requirements, evaluate the service offerings of potential cloud providers. Look for providers that offer services aligned with your needs, such as compute, storage, databases, and specialized services like machine learning or IoT.

Consider the scalability, performance, and features of these services. Are they sufficient for your workloads, and can they accommodate your growth? Pay attention to the diversity and maturity of the service portfolio.

4.4.3 Pricing and Cost Analysis

Cost is a critical factor in selecting a cloud provider. Analyze the pricing models, cost structures, and billing options offered by providers. Consider the following:

- **Pricing Plans:** Determine whether the provider offers pricing plans that align with your budget and usage patterns. Common models include pay-as-you-go, reserved instances, and subscription plans.
- **Total Cost of Ownership (TCO):** Calculate the TCO of running your workloads on each cloud provider. Include factors such as compute, storage, data transfer, and support costs.
- **Cost Optimization:** Assess the availability of cost optimization tools and recommendations to help you control and reduce cloud expenses.
- **Potential Discounts:** Check for discounts or cost-saving opportunities for long-term commitments or usage commitments.

4.4.4 Security and Compliance

Security and compliance are non-negotiable aspects of cloud computing. Evaluate the security measures and compliance certifications of potential providers:

- **Security Features:** Assess the provider's security capabilities, including encryption, identity and access management (IAM), and network security.
- **Data Protection:** Investigate data protection mechanisms, backup and recovery options, and data residency choices.
- **Compliance Certifications:** Ensure that the provider complies with industry-specific certifications and regulatory requirements relevant to your organization.
- **Incident Response:** Review the provider's incident response and recovery procedures in the event of security breaches or service interruptions.

4.4.5 Ecosystem and Integration

Consider the ecosystem and integration capabilities of the cloud provider:

- **Partners and Third-Party Integrations:** Evaluate the provider's ecosystem of partners and third-party integrations. A rich ecosystem can extend the functionality of your cloud resources.
- **Developer Support:** Look for comprehensive developer resources, including documentation, SDKs, and a vibrant developer community.
- **Interoperability:** Assess the provider's support for interoperability with other cloud providers or on-premises infrastructure. Avoid vendor lock-in when possible.

4.4.6 Global Reach and Support

If your organization operates internationally or targets specific regions, assess the global reach and customer support of potential providers:

- **Data Center Locations:** Ensure that the provider has data centers in regions that align with your target audience and compliance needs.
- **Content Delivery:** Check for the availability of content delivery networks (CDNs) to optimize content delivery worldwide.
- **Customer Support:** Evaluate the quality of customer support, including documentation, response times, and support tiers.

4.4.7 Test and Experiment

Before committing to a cloud provider, take advantage of trial periods or free tiers to test their services. Create a proof of concept or pilot project to assess how well the provider's offerings align with your requirements.

Experimenting with the provider's services in a real-world scenario can provide valuable insights into their usability, performance, and compatibility with your workloads.

4.4.8 Consider Long-Term Viability

Assess the long-term viability and stability of the cloud provider. Consider factors such as their financial health, track record, and commitment to innovation. A provider with a proven track record of investment in infrastructure and services is more likely to support your organization's growth.

4.4.9 Review and Reassess

Cloud provider services change, and new offerings emerge regularly. It's crucial to periodically review your cloud provider choices to ensure they continue to align with your evolving needs and goals.

By following this structured approach, you can systematically evaluate cloud providers and select the one that best aligns with your organization's unique requirements and aspirations in the cloud.

5: GETTING STARTED WITH CLOUD

5.1 Creating a Cloud Account

Before you can start using cloud services, you'll need to create an account with a cloud provider. This account serves as your gateway to the cloud, allowing you to access and manage cloud resources. We'll go through the process of creating a cloud account, using Amazon Web Services (AWS) as an example. Keep in mind that the specific steps may vary slightly depending on the cloud provider you choose, but the general principles remain similar.

5.1.1 Choose Your Cloud Provider

The first step in creating a cloud account is choosing the cloud provider that aligns with your needs. As you learned in previous chapters, major cloud providers like AWS, Microsoft Azure, and Google Cloud offer a wide range of services and global infrastructure. To get started, visit the website of your chosen cloud provider.

5.1.2 Sign-Up Process

Once you're on the cloud provider's website, you'll typically find a "Sign-Up" or "Create Account" option. Click on this option to initiate the account creation process. Here are the general steps involved:

Step 1: Account Information

- **Email Address:** Provide a valid email address that you'll use for your cloud account. This email will be associated with your cloud resources and communications from the cloud provider.
- **Password:** Create a strong and secure password for your account. Ensure it meets the provider's password requirements, which often include a mix of uppercase letters, lowercase letters, numbers, and special characters.

Step 2: Contact Information

- **Full Name:** Enter your full name as it appears on your identification documents.
- **Phone Number:** Provide a valid phone number. This can be used for account recovery and verification purposes.

Step 3: Payment Information

- **Credit Card Information:** You may need to provide credit card details. This information is used to verify your identity and set up billing for any services you use. Some cloud providers offer a free tier with limited resources that doesn't require payment information.

Step 4: Verification

- **Identity Verification:** To prevent fraud, the cloud provider may ask you to verify your identity. This can involve receiving a verification code via email or SMS and entering it on the website.

Step 5: Accept Terms and Conditions

- **Read and Accept:** Review the terms of service, privacy policy, and any other agreements presented by the cloud provider. Accept them if you agree with the terms.

Step 6: Account Creation

- **Confirmation:** Once you've completed all the required steps, you'll receive a confirmation that your account has been created.

5.1.3 Accessing the Cloud Console

After creating your cloud account, you'll gain access to the cloud provider's console or dashboard. This is a web-based interface where you can manage and configure cloud resources. The console is your control center for all things cloud-related, from launching virtual machines to managing storage and databases.

Logging In: To access the console, return to the cloud provider's website and click on the "Sign-In" or "Log In" option. Enter the email address and password you used during account creation.

Multi-Factor Authentication (MFA): For added security, consider enabling multi-factor authentication (MFA) if your cloud provider offers it. MFA requires you to enter a one-time code sent to your mobile device or generated by a mobile app in addition to your password.

Congratulations, you've successfully created a cloud account and gained access to the cloud console!

5.2 Setting Up Your First Virtual Machine

Now that you have created your cloud account and gained access to the cloud console, it's time to take your first steps in the cloud by setting up a virtual machine (VM). A virtual machine is a software emulation of a physical computer, allowing you to run various operating systems and applications in a virtualized environment. Remember that the steps may vary slightly depending on your chosen cloud provider, but the fundamental concepts remain consistent.

5.2.1 Accessing the Cloud Console

Before you can create a virtual machine, log in to your cloud provider's console using the credentials you set up during the account creation process. Once you're logged in, you'll be greeted by the dashboard or console homepage.

5.2.2 Navigating to the Compute Section

To create a virtual machine, you'll typically need to navigate to the "Compute" or "EC2" (Elastic Compute Cloud) section of the console. The specific terminology and layout may vary, but you'll generally find this section under "Services" or a similar menu.

5.2.3 Launching a Virtual Machine

Here are the general steps to launch a virtual machine:

Step 1: Choose "Launch Instance"

- Click on "Launch Instance" or a similar option to begin the VM creation process. You'll be presented with a series of steps to configure your VM.

Step 2: Choose an Amazon Machine Image (AMI)

- An AMI is a pre-configured template that includes an operating system and often additional software. Select an AMI that suits your needs. Common choices include Linux distributions like Ubuntu or CentOS and Windows Server versions.

Step 3: Choose an Instance Type

- Instances come in various sizes, each with different CPU, memory, and storage capacities. Choose the instance type that aligns with your workload requirements and budget.

Step 4: Configure Instance Details

- Configure additional settings like the number of instances to launch, networking options, and IAM (Identity and Access Management) roles if needed.

Step 5: Add Storage

- Specify the storage requirements for your VM, including the root volume size and any additional data volumes.

Step 6: Add Tags (Optional)

- You can add tags to your instances for better organization and management. Tags are key-value pairs that help you identify resources.

Step 7: Configure Security Groups

- Security groups act as virtual firewalls for your VM. Define inbound and outbound rules to control traffic to and from your VM.

Step 8: Review and Launch

- Review your instance configuration to ensure it meets your requirements. If everything looks good, click "Launch."

Step 9: Create a Key Pair (if applicable)

- If you're launching a Linux-based instance, you may need to create a key pair. This key pair is used to securely access your VM through SSH. Be sure to download and securely store the private key file.

Step 10: Launch Instances

- Confirm the launch by selecting the key pair (if applicable) and clicking "Launch Instances." Your virtual machine will now be provisioned and launched.

5.2.4 Accessing Your Virtual Machine

Once your virtual machine is running, you'll want to access it. Here's how:

SSH (Linux)

- If you're using a Linux-based VM, you can access it using SSH. Use the private key file you downloaded earlier during the key pair creation process.

Remote Desktop (Windows)

- For Windows-based VMs, you can access them using Remote Desktop Protocol (RDP). You'll need the username and password you set during the instance launch process.

Congratulations! You've successfully set up your first virtual machine in the cloud. You now have a virtualized environment that you can use to run applications, host websites, or perform various tasks.

5.3 Cloud Management Interfaces (Web Console, CLI)

Managing your cloud resources effectively requires access to user-friendly interfaces and tools that provide flexibility and control. Cloud providers offer two primary interfaces for managing resources: the web-based console and the command-line interface (CLI).

5.3.1 Web Console

The web console, often referred to as the management console or dashboard, is a user-friendly, graphical interface provided by cloud providers for managing cloud resources. Here are some key aspects of the web console:

1. Intuitive Interface: The web console typically features a user-friendly and intuitive graphical interface that doesn't require extensive technical expertise. It's an excellent choice for beginners and users who prefer a visual approach to managing resources.

2. Resource Visualization: It provides a visual representation of your cloud resources, making it easy to see and interact with virtual machines, storage, databases, and other services. You can often view and manage resources by navigating through menus and dashboards.

3. Resource Creation and Configuration: The web console allows you to create and configure cloud resources with ease. You can launch virtual machines, set up databases, configure networking, and manage security groups through point-and-click actions.

4. Monitoring and Metrics: You can use the console to monitor the health and performance of your resources. It provides dashboards and metrics for tracking CPU usage, network traffic, and more.

5. Role-Based Access Control: Most web consoles support role-based access control (RBAC), allowing you to grant specific permissions to users or groups. This helps ensure that users have the right level of access to resources.

6. Cross-Platform Access: The web console is accessible from any web browser, making it platform-independent. You can manage your cloud resources from Windows, macOS, Linux, or even mobile devices.

7. Troubleshooting and Support: The console often provides tools for troubleshooting issues, accessing support documentation, and contacting customer support if needed.

5.3.2 Command-Line Interface (CLI)

While the web console is user-friendly and accessible, the command-line interface (CLI) offers a more powerful and scriptable way to manage cloud resources. Here are some key aspects of the CLI:

1. Automation and Scripting: The CLI allows you to automate resource provisioning and management tasks using scripts. This is valuable for deploying and scaling resources programmatically.

2. Efficiency: Experienced users often find the CLI to be more efficient for repetitive tasks. With a few commands, you can create, configure, and manage multiple resources simultaneously.

3. Flexibility: The CLI provides fine-grained control over cloud resources, enabling you to customize configurations and settings in detail.

4. Compatibility: Most cloud providers offer CLI tools that are compatible with various operating systems, including Windows, macOS, and Linux. This ensures consistent management experiences across platforms.

5. Integration: The CLI can be integrated with other automation tools, such as Ansible, Terraform, and shell scripts, allowing for seamless orchestration of complex workflows.

6. Access Control: Access to the CLI can be controlled through access keys or tokens, providing a secure way to manage cloud resources.

7. Scalability: The CLI is well-suited for managing large-scale cloud environments and resources, especially in scenarios where resource creation and management must be automated.

5.3.3 Choosing the Right Interface

The choice between the web console and the CLI depends on your specific needs, preferences, and tasks:

- **Web Console:** Use the web console when you need a visual, point-and-click interface, especially for tasks like resource exploration, monitoring, and basic management. It's ideal for those who are new to cloud computing.
- **CLI:** Opt for the CLI when you require automation, scripting, and efficient management of resources, especially in complex and large-scale environments. It's well-suited for experienced users and DevOps professionals.

In practice, many cloud users leverage both interfaces, choosing the one that best suits the task at hand. Learning to use both the web console and the CLI can provide you with the flexibility to manage cloud resources effectively and efficiently.

5.4 Understanding Billing and Cost Management

One of the essential aspects of managing cloud resources effectively is understanding how cloud billing and cost management work. Cloud providers offer flexible pricing models, but without proper management, costs can quickly escalate.

5.4.1 Pay-as-You-Go vs. Reserved Instances

Cloud providers offer different pricing models, and understanding them is crucial for cost management:

1. Pay-as-You-Go (PAYG): This model charges you based on actual resource usage. You pay for the compute, storage, and other resources you consume. PAYG is flexible, as you can scale resources up or down as needed, but it can be more expensive if you have continuously running workloads.

2. Reserved Instances (RIs): RIs allow you to commit to a specific amount of resources for a defined period, typically one or three years. In return, you receive a significant discount compared to PAYG pricing. RIs are ideal for predictable workloads but require upfront commitment.

Understanding the balance between PAYG and RIs and when to use each can significantly impact your cloud costs.

5.4.2 Cost Allocation and Tagging

To track and manage costs effectively, cloud providers offer cost allocation and tagging features:

1. Cost Allocation: Cost allocation allows you to categorize your cloud expenses by project, department, or application. This helps you understand where your spending is concentrated.

2. Tagging: Tagging is a way to label resources with metadata, such as project names, environment (e.g., development, production), or owner information. Tags provide granularity for cost allocation.

Using these features, you can generate cost reports and gain insights into how resources contribute to your overall expenses.

5.4.3 Budgets and Alerts

Cloud providers offer budgeting and alerting tools to help you stay within your spending limits:

1. Budgets: Set up budgets to define spending thresholds for specific projects or departments. You can track spending against these budgets over time.

2. Alerts: Configure alerts that trigger when spending exceeds predefined thresholds. Alerts can be sent via email, SMS, or other notification methods.

Budgets and alerts are crucial for proactive cost management, allowing you to identify and address cost overruns promptly.

5.4.4 Cost Optimization Tools

Cloud providers offer cost optimization tools and recommendations to help you reduce expenses:

1. Right-Sizing: Right-sizing involves matching resource types and sizes to your actual workload requirements. Use tools to identify over-provisioned or underutilized resources.

2. Autoscaling: Implement autoscaling to dynamically adjust resources based on demand. Autoscaling helps you avoid over-provisioning during traffic spikes.

3. Reserved Instances (RIs): Consider RIs for workloads with predictable usage patterns. RIs offer cost savings in exchange for upfront commitment.

4. Spot Instances: Spot instances allow you to use spare capacity at a significantly lower cost. They are suitable for fault-tolerant and flexible workloads.

5. Serverless: Consider serverless computing models (e.g., AWS Lambda, Azure Functions) for certain workloads. You pay only for the compute resources used during execution.

6. Cloud Native Services: Leverage cloud-native services like managed databases and storage to offload management overhead and reduce costs.

Cost optimization is an ongoing process, and regular analysis of your cloud resources and usage patterns is essential.

5.4.5 Security and Compliance Costs

Don't overlook security and compliance costs when managing your cloud budget. Security measures, data encryption, and compliance certifications may incur additional expenses. Ensure that you budget for these critical aspects to protect your cloud resources and data.

5.4.6 Continuous Monitoring and Review

Effective cost management is an ongoing practice. Regularly monitor your cloud costs, review budgets, and analyze spending patterns. Consider conducting cost optimization reviews at predefined intervals to identify areas for improvement.

5.4.7 Cloud Cost Management Services

Additionally, some third-party tools and services specialize in cloud cost management and optimization. These tools provide advanced analytics, automation, and recommendations to help you control and reduce cloud expenses further.

6: CLOUD SECURITY AND COMPLIANCE

6.1 Cloud Security Concerns

Security in the cloud is a shared responsibility between you and your cloud service provider. While cloud providers invest heavily in securing their infrastructure, you, as the cloud user, have a crucial role to play in securing your own workloads, applications, and data.

6.1.1 Data Breaches

Data breaches are one of the most significant security concerns in the cloud. These breaches involve unauthorized access to sensitive data, often resulting in its theft or exposure. Data breaches can lead to severe consequences, including financial losses, reputational damage, and regulatory fines. Key factors contributing to data breaches in the cloud include:

- **Inadequate Access Controls:** Weak or misconfigured access controls can allow unauthorized users to access data.
- **Data Encryption:** Insufficient encryption measures may expose data during transmission or while at rest.
- **Credential Compromises:** Stolen or weak credentials can grant unauthorized access to cloud resources.

6.1.2 Identity and Access Management (IAM) Issues

Effective **Identity and Access Management (IAM)** is critical in the cloud. IAM concerns revolve around the management of user identities, roles, and permissions. Common IAM issues include:

- **Improper Permissions:** Assigning excessive or unnecessary permissions to users or resources can create security vulnerabilities.
- **Inadequate Authentication:** Weak authentication mechanisms can lead to unauthorized access.
- **Account Compromises:** User accounts may be compromised through techniques like phishing or credential theft.

6.1.3 Insider Threats

Insider threats occur when individuals within an organization misuse their access privileges to compromise security. These individuals may be employees, contractors, or partners. Insider threats can take various forms, including data theft, sabotage, or espionage. Detecting and mitigating insider threats in the cloud is challenging but essential.

6.1.4 Insecure APIs

Application Programming Interfaces (APIs) are used for communication between cloud services and applications. Insecure or poorly configured APIs can be exploited by attackers to gain unauthorized access to data or resources. Ensuring API security is crucial, including proper authentication and authorization mechanisms.

6.1.5 Regulatory Compliance

Different industries and regions have specific **regulatory compliance** requirements related to data protection, privacy, and security. Failing to comply with these regulations can lead to legal consequences, fines, and reputational damage. Cloud users must understand and address compliance requirements relevant to their industry and geographic location.

6.1.6 Shared Infrastructure Vulnerabilities

Cloud providers use shared infrastructure to serve multiple customers. While providers implement strong isolation between tenants, **shared infrastructure vulnerabilities** can still pose a risk. These vulnerabilities may allow one tenant to impact or compromise the resources of another. Understanding the provider's security measures and implementing additional protections is crucial.

6.1.7 DDoS Attacks

Distributed Denial of Service (DDoS) attacks are a threat in the cloud, where attackers attempt to overwhelm a target with a flood of traffic, causing service disruption. Cloud providers offer DDoS protection services, but users must configure and monitor them effectively.

6.1.8 Lack of Visibility and Control

The **lack of visibility and control** over cloud resources can be a concern. In traditional on-premises environments, organizations have greater visibility and control, while the cloud offers more abstracted and automated services. Ensuring proper monitoring, logging, and auditing practices is essential to maintain visibility and control.

6.2 Authentication and Access Control

Effective **authentication** and **access control** are foundational components of cloud security. They are essential for verifying the identities of users and controlling their access to resources and data within a cloud environment.

6.2.1 Authentication

Authentication is the process of verifying the identity of a user or system attempting to access a resource. In the cloud, authentication ensures that only authorized users and applications can interact with cloud services and data. Here are key considerations:

1. Multi-Factor Authentication (MFA): Implement **Multi-Factor Authentication (MFA)** wherever possible. MFA requires users to provide two or more types of authentication factors, such as a password and a one-time code sent to their mobile device. This significantly enhances security.

2. Strong Password Policies: Enforce strong password policies that require complex, unique passwords for user accounts. Regularly prompt users to update their passwords, and consider using password managers.

3. Single Sign-On (SSO): Consider implementing **Single Sign-On (SSO)** solutions. SSO allows users to access multiple services with a single set of credentials, simplifying authentication while maintaining security.

4. OAuth and OpenID Connect: Use industry-standard protocols like **OAuth** and **OpenID Connect** for secure authorization and authentication of applications and APIs. These protocols are widely adopted and provide strong security features.

6.2.2 Access Control

Access control involves defining and managing who has access to specific resources and what actions they can perform on those resources. Effective access control helps prevent unauthorized access and reduces the attack surface. Here are key access control practices:

1. Role-Based Access Control (RBAC): Implement **Role-Based Access Control (RBAC)** to assign permissions to users based on their roles and responsibilities. Assign the principle of least privilege, granting users only the permissions they need to perform their tasks.

2. Resource-Level Permissions: Define resource-level permissions to control access to individual resources, such as virtual machines, databases, and storage objects. Granular permissions offer fine-grained control.

3. Identity Federation: Use **identity federation** to allow users from trusted external identity providers (e.g., Active Directory) to access cloud resources seamlessly. This enhances security and simplifies user management.

4. Access Policies: Create access policies that define rules for access to specific resources and services. Policies can be used to enforce security standards and compliance requirements.

5. Regular Auditing: Implement regular auditing and monitoring of access controls. Monitor for unusual or unauthorized access patterns and take action promptly.

6.2.3 Key Management and Encryption

To enhance authentication and access control, consider the use of encryption and key management:

1. Data Encryption: Encrypt data both in transit and at rest. Use protocols like **TLS/SSL** for data in transit and encryption mechanisms provided by cloud services for data at rest.

2. Key Management: Securely manage encryption keys. Cloud providers offer **Key Management Services (KMS)** for generating, storing, and rotating encryption keys. Properly configure and protect key access.

3. Bring Your Own Key (BYOK): Some cloud providers allow you to bring your encryption keys. BYOK gives you greater control over key management and security.

Implementing strong authentication and access control measures, including MFA, RBAC, encryption, and key management, significantly enhances the security of your cloud environment. These practices help ensure that only authorized users and applications have access to sensitive resources and data, reducing the risk of security breaches.

6.3 Data Encryption in the Cloud

Data encryption is a fundamental component of cloud security, ensuring the confidentiality and integrity of your sensitive information. In the cloud, data can be in transit (moving between cloud services and devices) or at rest (stored on servers or storage systems). To protect your data effectively, it's essential to employ encryption measures for both scenarios.

6.3.1 Encryption in Transit

Encryption in transit focuses on securing data while it's being transmitted between different points within your cloud infrastructure. This includes data traveling between your local device and the cloud provider's services, as well as data transferred between various cloud services. Here are key considerations:

1. Transport Layer Security (TLS) / Secure Sockets Layer (SSL): Implement **Transport Layer Security (TLS)** or its predecessor **Secure Sockets Layer (SSL)** for encrypting data in transit. These protocols ensure that data transmitted between clients and cloud services remains confidential and tamper-proof.

2. HTTPS: Use **HTTPS (HTTP Secure)** for web applications and websites hosted in the cloud. HTTPS encrypts the data exchanged between users' web browsers and web servers, protecting sensitive information such as login credentials and payment details.

3. VPNs: Utilize Virtual Private Networks (VPNs) for secure communication between your on-premises network and cloud resources. VPNs establish encrypted tunnels to safeguard data during transmission.

4. Encrypted APIs: When building or interacting with cloud-based applications and services, ensure that they use encrypted APIs (e.g., REST over HTTPS) for data exchange. Encryption should be a standard practice in your application development.

6.3.2 Encryption at Rest

Encryption at rest focuses on safeguarding data when it's stored in cloud databases, file storage, or other data repositories. Even within a cloud provider's data centers, data encryption at rest is essential to protect against unauthorized access, including physical security breaches. Here are key practices:

1. Server-Side Encryption (SSE): Most cloud providers offer **Server-Side Encryption (SSE)** for data at rest. SSE automatically encrypts data before it's written to disk and decrypts it when read. There are typically different SSE modes, such as SSE-S3 for object storage and SSE-KMS for key management.

2. Bring Your Own Key (BYOK): Consider using **Bring Your Own Key (BYOK)** services provided by cloud providers. BYOK allows you to manage and control your encryption keys, providing an additional layer of security and compliance.

3. Data Classification: Implement data classification practices to identify sensitive data. Prioritize encrypting highly sensitive data, such as personally identifiable information (PII) or financial records.

4. Database Encryption: For databases in the cloud, enable database-level encryption to protect data at rest. This includes encrypting tables, columns, and backups.

5. Key Management: Properly manage encryption keys to ensure they are protected. Cloud providers often offer Key Management Services (KMS) for secure key storage and rotation.

6. Compliance Requirements: Understand and comply with industry-specific regulations and data protection laws that may require data encryption at rest, such as the General Data Protection Regulation (GDPR) in Europe.

7. Logging and Auditing: Enable logging and auditing of access to encrypted data. Monitoring access to encrypted data helps identify and respond to security incidents.

Encrypting data at rest and in transit is a crucial aspect of cloud security. It provides a strong layer of defense, ensuring that even if data is compromised, it remains unreadable without the appropriate decryption keys. By implementing encryption best practices, you enhance the confidentiality and integrity of your data in the cloud.

6.4 Compliance and Regulatory Considerations

Various industries and regions have specific rules and regulations governing data protection, privacy, and security. Whether you're a healthcare provider subject to the Health Insurance Portability and Accountability Act (HIPAA) or a financial institution complying with the Payment Card Industry Data Security Standard (PCI DSS), cloud compliance is a complex but necessary aspect of cloud security.

6.4.1 Industry-Specific Regulations

Different industries have unique compliance requirements that cloud users must address. Here are a few examples:

1. Healthcare (HIPAA): Healthcare organizations must adhere to the **Health Insurance Portability and Accountability Act (HIPAA)** when storing, transmitting, or processing patient health information (PHI) in the cloud. HIPAA mandates strict controls over access, audit trails, and data encryption.

2. Financial Services (PCI DSS): Financial institutions handling credit card data must comply with the **Payment Card Industry Data Security Standard (PCI DSS)**. This standard dictates security measures such as encryption, access controls, and regular security assessments.

3. Government (FedRAMP, FISMA): Cloud providers serving government agencies in the United States must meet the requirements of the **Federal Risk and Authorization Management Program (FedRAMP)** and the **Federal Information Security Management Act (FISMA)**.

4. GDPR and Data Privacy: The **General Data Protection Regulation (GDPR)** in Europe imposes strict data protection and privacy requirements. Organizations worldwide must comply when handling personal data of EU citizens.

6.4.2 International Data Transfer

When using cloud services, especially across borders, data sovereignty and international data transfer rules become significant concerns. Some countries have strict laws governing the storage and processing of data within their borders. To navigate this:

1. Data Residency: Choose cloud providers with data centers in regions that align with your compliance requirements. Many cloud providers offer region-specific services.

2. Privacy Shield and SCCs: The EU-U.S. Privacy Shield and Standard Contractual Clauses (SCCs) are mechanisms for transferring personal data from the European Union to the United States and other countries, ensuring adequate data protection.

3. Data Impact Assessments: Perform data impact assessments to understand the data flow within your cloud environment and identify potential compliance risks.

6.4.3 Cloud Provider Compliance and Shared Responsibility

Understanding the shared responsibility model with your cloud provider is essential. While cloud providers maintain the security of their infrastructure, you are responsible for securing your applications, data, and configurations. Cloud providers often offer compliance documentation and attestations to help you meet regulatory requirements.

1. Compliance Documentation: Review your cloud provider's compliance documentation, including audit reports and certifications like SOC 2, ISO 27001, or FedRAMP. These demonstrate the provider's commitment to security and compliance.

2. Access Controls: Ensure you have strong identity and access controls in place. Implement role-based access control (RBAC) to manage permissions effectively.

3. Encryption: Encrypt data both in transit and at rest, and use secure key management practices.

4. Auditing and Monitoring: Implement auditing and monitoring to track access to sensitive data and detect potential security incidents.

5. Incident Response Plan: Develop an incident response plan that includes actions to take in case of a security breach to meet compliance reporting requirements.

6.4.4 Continuous Compliance Monitoring

Achieving and maintaining compliance is an ongoing process. Continuously monitor your cloud environment for compliance violations and security threats. Automated compliance monitoring tools can help ensure that your cloud resources remain compliant with regulations and industry standards.

Compliance in the cloud is a shared responsibility between you and your cloud provider. By understanding your industry-specific requirements, international data transfer rules, and the shared responsibility model, you can build a strong compliance posture in the cloud. Regularly review and update your compliance practices to adapt to changing regulations and ensure the security of your cloud environment.

6.5 Best Practices for Cloud Security

Securing your cloud environment requires a proactive approach and a combination of best practices that address a wide range of security threats and challenges. Implementing these practices not only safeguards your cloud resources but also helps you maintain data privacy and regulatory compliance. Here are some essential best practices for cloud security:

6.5.1 Use Strong Authentication and Access Control

1. Multi-Factor Authentication (MFA): Enforce the use of **Multi-Factor Authentication (MFA)** for all user accounts. This adds an extra layer of security by requiring users to provide multiple forms of verification before granting access.

2. Role-Based Access Control (RBAC): Implement **Role-Based Access Control (RBAC)** to manage permissions effectively. Assign permissions based on job roles, and regularly review and update permissions as needed.

3. Least Privilege Principle: Follow the principle of least privilege, granting users and applications the minimum level of access necessary to perform their tasks. This reduces the attack surface.

6.5.2 Encrypt Data

4. Encryption at Rest: Encrypt sensitive data at rest using cloud provider encryption services. Ensure that encryption keys are managed securely.

5. Encryption in Transit: Use encryption protocols such as **TLS/SSL** to encrypt data in transit, ensuring that data transmitted between clients and cloud services is secure.

6.5.3 Regularly Update and Patch

6. Regular Software Updates: Keep all software, including operating systems, applications, and cloud services, up to date with the latest security patches. Vulnerabilities in outdated software can be exploited by attackers.

6.5.4 Monitor and Audit

7. Logging and Monitoring: Implement comprehensive logging and monitoring of your cloud resources. Set up alerts for suspicious activities and security incidents, and regularly review logs for anomalies.

8. Security Information and Event Management (SIEM): Consider using a Security Information and Event Management (SIEM) system to aggregate and analyze security data from various sources, providing insights into security events and trends.

6.5.5 Backup and Disaster Recovery

9. Regular Backups: Implement regular automated backups of your critical data and configurations. Ensure that backups are stored securely and can be restored when needed.

10. Disaster Recovery Plan: Develop a comprehensive disaster recovery plan that includes procedures for data recovery, service restoration, and communication in the event of a major incident.

6.5.6 Implement Security Policies

11. Security Policies: Establish and communicate clear security policies and procedures to your organization's staff and cloud users. Ensure that security policies align with industry best practices and compliance requirements.

12. Incident Response Plan: Create an incident response plan that outlines the steps to take in the event of a security incident. Test and update the plan regularly.

6.5.7 Security Awareness Training

13. Security Training: Provide security awareness training to all employees and users who interact with your cloud environment. Educate them on security risks, best practices, and how to recognize and report potential threats.

6.5.8 Third-Party Security Assessment

14. Third-Party Services: If you use third-party services or applications in your cloud environment, assess their security practices and ensure they align with your security requirements.

6.5.9 Continuous Improvement

15. Security Reviews: Conduct regular security reviews and assessments of your cloud environment. Identify areas for improvement and take corrective actions promptly.

16. Automation: Leverage automation for security tasks, such as vulnerability scanning, threat detection, and compliance checks, to maintain consistent security across your cloud infrastructure.

By incorporating these best practices into your cloud security strategy, you can establish a robust security posture that protects your cloud resources from a wide range of threats.

7: CLOUD DEPLOYMENT AND MIGRATION

7.1 Moving to the Cloud

The decision to move to the cloud is not just about technology; it's a strategic business move with far-reaching implications. As organizations increasingly adopt cloud computing, understanding the motivations, benefits, and considerations for migrating to the cloud is essential.

7.1.1 Why Move to the Cloud?

1. Cost Optimization: Cloud computing offers cost advantages by eliminating the need for on-premises hardware and reducing operational expenses. Pay-as-you-go pricing models allow organizations to scale resources up or down based on demand.

2. Scalability: The cloud provides the ability to scale resources rapidly to meet changing business needs. This agility is particularly beneficial for businesses with fluctuating workloads.

3. Accessibility and Flexibility: Cloud services are accessible from anywhere with an internet connection, providing flexibility for remote work and global collaboration.

4. Innovation: Cloud platforms offer a range of services, including AI, machine learning, and data analytics, enabling organizations to innovate and develop new digital solutions quickly.

5. Security and Compliance: Cloud providers invest heavily in security, and many offer compliance certifications. Leveraging their expertise can enhance security and help meet regulatory requirements.

6. Disaster Recovery: Cloud-based disaster recovery solutions provide robust backup and recovery capabilities, ensuring business continuity in case of data loss or system failures.

7.1.2 Cloud Adoption Considerations

1. Cloud Readiness Assessment: Evaluate your organization's readiness for cloud adoption. Assess factors like existing infrastructure, skillsets, and the cultural shift required.

2. Data Classification: Understand your data's sensitivity and compliance requirements. Determine which data can be moved to the cloud and which should remain on-premises or in a private cloud.

3. Migration Strategy: Choose a migration strategy that aligns with your goals. Strategies include rehosting (lift and shift), refactoring (rearchitecting), replatforming (making minimal changes), and rebuilding (creating cloud-native apps).

4. Cloud Service Models: Decide which cloud service models (IaaS, PaaS, SaaS) best suit your needs. For more control and customization, IaaS may be appropriate, while SaaS offers ready-to-use applications.

5. Cloud Deployment Models: Consider public, private, or hybrid cloud deployment based on security, compliance, and performance requirements.

6. Training and Skill Development: Invest in training and skill development for your IT team to ensure they have the expertise to manage and optimize cloud resources effectively.

7. Vendor Selection: Choose a reputable cloud provider that aligns with your business goals, offers the required services, and complies with your industry's regulations.

7.1.3 Migration Challenges

While the cloud offers numerous benefits, the migration process can pose challenges:

1. Data Transfer: Moving large volumes of data to the cloud can be time-consuming and may require optimizing data transfer methods.

2. Application Compatibility: Legacy applications may require modifications or updates to run efficiently in the cloud.

3. Security Concerns: Ensuring the security of data and applications in the cloud is a top priority. Addressing security concerns is critical during migration.

4. Cost Management: While cloud computing can be cost-effective, improper resource provisioning and management can lead to unexpected expenses.

5. Compliance: Meeting regulatory and compliance requirements in the cloud requires careful planning and execution.

Successful cloud migration demands a well-defined strategy, thorough assessment, and skilled execution. It's not just about relocating data and applications; it's a strategic shift that can transform how your organization operates and competes in the digital age.

7.2 Migrating Existing Applications

One of the most common scenarios in cloud adoption is migrating existing applications to the cloud. Whether you have legacy applications running on on-premises servers or virtualized workloads in a data center, moving them to the cloud can unlock benefits like improved scalability, cost optimization, and enhanced accessibility. However, the process of migrating existing applications requires careful planning and execution.

7.2.1 Assessment and Planning

1. Application Inventory: Begin by creating an inventory of all the applications you intend to migrate. Understand their dependencies, data requirements, and criticality to your business operations.

2. Compatibility Check: Evaluate the compatibility of each application with the target cloud environment. Some applications may require modifications or updates to run smoothly in the cloud.

3. Data Considerations: Assess the data associated with each application. Determine how data will be migrated and whether any data transformations are necessary.

4. Migration Strategy: Choose an appropriate migration strategy based on your assessment. Common strategies include:

- **Rehosting (Lift and Shift):** This strategy involves moving applications and their dependencies to the cloud without making significant code changes. It's a quick way to get applications into the cloud but may not fully leverage cloud-native features.
- **Refactoring (Rearchitecting):** Refactoring involves making changes to the application's architecture to take advantage of cloud-native services. This approach can lead to improved performance and scalability.
- **Replatforming (Making Minimal Changes):** In this strategy, applications are modified slightly to run efficiently in

the cloud environment. It strikes a balance between speed and optimization.

- **Rebuilding (Creating Cloud-Native Apps):** In this approach, applications are rebuilt from the ground up to be cloud-native, utilizing microservices, serverless, and other cloud services.

7.2.2 Data Migration

1. Data Transfer Methods: Choose data transfer methods that align with your data volume and transfer speed requirements. Options include online transfers, offline data shipping, and data synchronization.

2. Data Transformation: If needed, perform data transformations to ensure that data is compatible with the target cloud platform and application versions.

3. Data Backup: Ensure that you have backups of your data before initiating the migration process. Data loss during migration can be mitigated by having a solid backup strategy in place.

7.2.3 Testing and Validation

1. Test Environments: Set up testing environments in the cloud to validate application functionality, performance, and security. Testing should encompass functional, load, and security testing.

2. Rollback Plan: Develop a rollback plan that outlines the steps to revert to the previous state in case the migration encounters issues that cannot be resolved quickly.

7.2.4 Execution and Optimization

1. Migration Execution: Execute the migration plan with careful coordination to minimize downtime and disruptions. Monitor the process closely and address any issues promptly.

2. Performance Optimization: After migration, optimize application performance in the cloud environment. Adjust resource allocation, fine-tune configurations, and leverage cloud-native services to enhance performance and cost-efficiency.

3. Cost Management: Continuously monitor and manage costs associated with running the migrated applications. Implement cost optimization strategies, such as reserved instances or autoscaling, to control expenses.

7.2.5 Post-Migration Support

1. Training and Documentation: Ensure that your IT team is trained in managing and maintaining applications in the cloud environment. Document processes, configurations, and best practices.

2. Security and Compliance: Review and update security and compliance measures to align with the cloud environment. Regularly audit and assess your cloud infrastructure for vulnerabilities and compliance.

Migrating existing applications to the cloud can be a complex endeavor, but when executed with careful planning and consideration, it can lead to significant benefits. It's essential to follow a structured approach, assess each application's unique requirements, and continuously monitor and optimize the cloud environment for ongoing success.

7.3 Cloud-Native Development

In today's digital world, where agility, scalability, and innovation are paramount, cloud-native development has emerged as a transformative approach. Cloud-native applications are designed and built to leverage the full potential of cloud computing services and technologies. This approach empowers organizations to deliver software faster, adapt to changing demands, and capitalize on the benefits of the cloud.

7.3.1 Characteristics of Cloud-Native Applications

Cloud-native applications exhibit several key characteristics that set them apart from traditional, monolithic applications:

1. Microservices Architecture: Cloud-native applications are typically built using a **microservices architecture**, where the application is composed of small, loosely coupled services that can be developed, deployed, and scaled independently.

2. Containerization: Containers, such as those managed by Docker, are a fundamental building block of cloud-native development. They provide consistency in development, testing, and production environments.

3. DevOps and Continuous Integration/Continuous Deployment (CI/CD): Cloud-native development emphasizes **DevOps practices** and **CI/CD pipelines**, enabling rapid development, testing, and deployment of code changes.

4. Elasticity and Auto-Scaling: Cloud-native applications can automatically scale their resources up or down based on demand, optimizing cost and performance.

5. Resilience: They are designed with resilience in mind, using mechanisms like redundancy, failover, and graceful degradation to ensure uptime and availability.

6. Cloud-Native Services: These applications make extensive use of **cloud-native services** provided by cloud providers, such as managed databases, serverless functions, and AI/ML services.

7.3.2 Benefits of Cloud-Native Development

Adopting cloud-native development offers organizations numerous advantages:

1. Speed to Market: Cloud-native applications can be developed and deployed quickly, allowing organizations to respond rapidly to changing market conditions and customer demands.

2. Scalability: They can easily scale to handle increased workloads, ensuring a smooth user experience during periods of high demand.

3. Cost Efficiency: Cloud-native applications are cost-efficient, as they optimize resource usage and leverage cloud provider pricing models.

4. Innovation: Cloud-native development encourages innovation by enabling the rapid integration of new technologies and services.

5. Reliability: With built-in resilience and failover mechanisms, cloud-native applications are highly reliable and can maintain availability even in the face of failures.

7.3.3 Building Cloud-Native Applications

Building cloud-native applications involves a series of key practices:

1. Microservices: Design applications as a collection of small, independent microservices that can be developed and deployed separately.

2. Containers: Use containerization technologies like Docker to package and distribute applications and their dependencies.

3. Kubernetes: Leverage container orchestration platforms like Kubernetes to automate deployment, scaling, and management of containers.

4. Serverless Computing: Explore serverless computing platforms like AWS Lambda, Azure Functions, or Google Cloud Functions to build event-driven, scalable components of your application.

5. DevOps and CI/CD: Implement DevOps practices, continuous integration, and continuous deployment to streamline development, testing, and deployment workflows.

6. Cloud-Native Services: Take advantage of cloud-native services provided by your chosen cloud provider to offload infrastructure management and focus on application development.

7. Monitoring and Observability: Implement robust monitoring and observability solutions to gain insights into the performance and health of your cloud-native applications.

7.3.4 Challenges of Cloud-Native Development

While cloud-native development offers significant benefits, it also presents challenges:

1. Complexity: Managing a microservices-based architecture can be complex, requiring expertise in container orchestration and service discovery.

2. Cultural Shift: Adopting cloud-native practices often necessitates a cultural shift within organizations, emphasizing collaboration, automation, and continuous improvement.

3. Skills Gap: Developers and operations teams may need to acquire new skills in areas like containerization, Kubernetes, and serverless computing.

4. Security: Securing microservices and containers, as well as ensuring compliance, can be challenging and requires careful consideration.

5. Vendor Lock-In: Leveraging cloud-native services can lead to vendor lock-in, making it challenging to switch cloud providers.

7.4 Testing and Deployment Strategies

Effective testing and deployment practices enable organizations to roll out new features, updates, and bug fixes efficiently, while minimizing disruptions to end-users.

7.4.1 Continuous Integration and Continuous Deployment (CI/CD)

Continuous Integration (CI) and **Continuous Deployment (CD)** are foundational practices for cloud-native development. They streamline the process of code development, testing, and deployment:

1. Continuous Integration (CI): Developers regularly integrate their code changes into a shared repository. Automated tests are run to ensure that new code doesn't introduce defects. CI helps catch issues early in the development cycle.

2. Continuous Deployment (CD): After successful CI, CD automates the process of deploying code changes to production. This can be done gradually, allowing for canary releases or blue-green deployments to minimize risk.

7.4.2 Testing Strategies

Effective testing strategies are essential for ensuring that applications function as expected in the cloud environment:

1. Unit Testing: Developers write unit tests to validate the functionality of individual code components or functions. Automated unit tests help catch bugs during development.

2. Integration Testing: Integration tests check how different components or services interact with each other. They ensure that the integrated parts of the application work seamlessly.

3. Load and Performance Testing: Load testing evaluates how well an application performs under a specific load, helping identify bottlenecks and performance issues. Performance testing focuses on optimizing the application's response time and resource utilization.

4. Security Testing: Security testing assesses the application's vulnerability to threats and attacks. This includes vulnerability scanning, penetration testing, and code analysis for security vulnerabilities.

5. Automated Testing: Automated testing, including the use of testing frameworks and tools, allows for faster and more consistent testing processes. Automated tests can be integrated into CI/CD pipelines.

7.4.3 Deployment Strategies

Effective deployment strategies ensure that code changes are rolled out smoothly and can be rolled back if issues arise:

1. Blue-Green Deployment: In a blue-green deployment, two identical environments (blue and green) are maintained. The current production environment (blue) continues to serve users while the new version is deployed to the green environment. Once the green environment is tested and validated, traffic is switched to it.

2. Canary Deployment: Canary deployments involve rolling out new code changes to a subset of users or servers before making it available to the entire user base. This approach allows organizations to detect issues early and mitigate risks.

3. Feature Toggles (Feature Flags): Feature toggles allow developers to enable or disable specific features in production without modifying the code. This enables controlled feature releases and the ability to roll back if needed.

4. Rollback Plans: Always have rollback plans in place. If issues are detected after a deployment, a well-defined rollback procedure can quickly revert to the previous stable version.

7.4.4 Infrastructure as Code (IaC)

Infrastructure as Code (IaC) is a fundamental practice for managing and deploying cloud infrastructure. IaC allows you to define and provision infrastructure resources programmatically. Tools like Terraform, AWS CloudFormation, and Azure Resource Manager enable the automation of infrastructure provisioning, ensuring consistency and repeatability.

7.4.5 Testing in Production

Testing in production involves continuously monitoring and testing applications and infrastructure in the production environment. This approach allows organizations to detect issues that may only manifest under real-world conditions. Techniques such as canary releases and feature flags facilitate safe testing in production.

8: CLOUD MANAGEMENT AND OPTIMIZATION

8.1 Cloud Resource Management

Effective management of cloud resources is essential for maintaining control, optimizing costs, and ensuring the reliability of your cloud infrastructure. In the dynamic cloud environment, where resources can be provisioned and scaled rapidly, managing these assets efficiently becomes a critical task.

8.1.1 Resource Provisioning and Governance

1. Resource Provisioning: Cloud resource provisioning involves creating and allocating resources such as virtual machines, databases, storage, and network components. This process should align with your organization's needs, ensuring that resources are available when and where they are required.

2. Resource Tagging: Implement a robust tagging strategy to label resources with metadata, making it easier to categorize, track, and allocate costs. Tags can help in identifying ownership, purpose, and project associations for resources.

3. Governance Policies: Establish governance policies to define resource provisioning rules, cost allocation, access controls, and compliance requirements. These policies should be well-documented and enforced consistently.

8.1.2 Cost Management

1. Cost Visibility: Gain visibility into your cloud costs by using cloud cost management tools and dashboards. Understand where your spending is allocated and identify cost drivers.

2. Budgeting: Set and monitor budgets to control your cloud spending. Budgets help you prevent cost overruns and align spending with your organization's financial objectives.

3. Cost Allocation: Implement cost allocation methods to attribute cloud costs to specific teams, projects, or departments. This enables chargeback or showback processes, making individuals or teams accountable for their cloud usage.

4. Cost Optimization: Continuously optimize your cloud spending by identifying idle resources, rightsizing instances, and leveraging reserved instances or savings plans to reduce costs.

8.1.3 Performance Monitoring

1. Monitoring Tools: Use cloud-native monitoring tools and third-party solutions to gain insights into the performance and health of your cloud resources. Monitor key performance metrics such as CPU utilization, network traffic, and latency.

2. Alerts and Notifications: Set up alerts and notifications to proactively detect and respond to performance issues. Alerts can trigger automated actions or notifications to the appropriate personnel.

3. Scaling Strategies: Implement auto-scaling policies to dynamically adjust resource capacity based on workload demands.

This ensures that your applications perform optimally without overprovisioning resources.

8.1.4 Security and Compliance

1. Security Policies: Define and enforce security policies that cover data protection, identity and access management, network security, and threat detection. Regularly review and update security policies to address emerging threats.

2. Compliance Management: Ensure that your cloud infrastructure complies with industry-specific regulations and standards. Cloud providers offer compliance certifications for various frameworks, which can simplify the compliance process.

3. Security Audits: Conduct regular security audits and assessments to identify vulnerabilities and security gaps. Remediate any issues promptly to maintain a secure cloud environment.

8.1.5 Resource Optimization

1. Rightsizing: Continuously review resource utilization and rightsize instances to match workload requirements. Downsizing underutilized resources and upgrading when needed can lead to significant cost savings.

2. Cloud-Native Features: Leverage cloud-native features and services to optimize resource usage. Examples include serverless computing for event-driven workloads and managed databases for scalability and performance.

3. Resource Lifecycle Management: Implement resource lifecycle policies to automate resource creation, scaling, and decommissioning. This helps prevent resource sprawl and associated costs.

Effective cloud resource management is an ongoing process that requires careful planning, monitoring, and optimization. By implementing these practices, you can maintain control over your cloud environment, optimize costs, ensure high performance, and uphold security and compliance standards.

8.2 Monitoring and Performance Optimization

Monitoring and optimizing the performance of your cloud resources is essential for delivering a seamless user experience, maintaining cost-efficiency, and ensuring the reliability of your applications.

8.2.1 Cloud Monitoring Fundamentals

1. Real-time Visibility: Cloud monitoring provides real-time visibility into the performance and health of your cloud resources. It enables you to proactively identify and address issues before they impact your applications.

2. Key Metrics: Monitor key metrics such as CPU utilization, memory usage, disk I/O, network latency, and error rates. These metrics provide insights into the health and performance of your cloud resources.

3. Alerts and Notifications: Set up alerts based on predefined thresholds or anomalies. When thresholds are breached or anomalies are detected, alerts notify your team or trigger automated actions for issue resolution.

8.2.2 Performance Optimization Strategies

1. Auto-Scaling: Implement auto-scaling policies that automatically adjust resource capacity based on workload demands. This ensures that your applications can handle traffic spikes without overprovisioning resources during periods of low demand.

2. Load Balancing: Use load balancers to distribute incoming traffic evenly across multiple instances. Load balancing improves application availability, fault tolerance, and scalability.

3. Content Delivery Networks (CDNs): Leverage CDNs to cache and deliver static content closer to end-users. CDNs reduce latency and improve the speed of content delivery, enhancing the user experience.

4. Caching: Implement caching mechanisms for frequently accessed data. Caching reduces the load on backend servers and speeds up response times for users.

5. Performance Testing: Conduct performance testing, including load testing and stress testing, to identify bottlenecks and optimize your application's performance under heavy loads.

8.2.3 Cloud-Native Monitoring Tools

1. Cloud Provider Monitoring Services: Cloud providers offer native monitoring services, such as AWS CloudWatch, Azure Monitor, and Google Cloud Monitoring, that provide insights into the health and performance of cloud resources.

2. Third-Party Monitoring Tools: Consider using third-party monitoring solutions like Prometheus, Grafana, New Relic, or Datadog for advanced monitoring capabilities, custom dashboards, and integrations with various cloud services.

3. Log Analysis: Utilize log analysis tools to collect and analyze logs from your applications and infrastructure. Log analysis helps in troubleshooting issues and identifying performance bottlenecks.

4. APM (Application Performance Monitoring): APM tools like AppDynamics and Dynatrace provide deep insights into application performance, including code-level diagnostics and transaction tracing.

8.2.4 Performance Optimization Best Practices

1. Regular Review: Continuously review monitoring data and performance metrics to identify trends and potential issues. Regular reviews enable proactive optimization.

2. Benchmarking: Benchmark your application's performance against industry standards and best practices. Benchmarking helps you set performance goals and measure your progress.

3. Resource Profiling: Use resource profiling tools to understand how your application consumes resources. Profiling helps pinpoint areas for optimization.

4. Security Considerations: Be mindful of security when optimizing performance. Ensure that optimization measures do not compromise security controls or introduce vulnerabilities.

5. Cost Optimization: While optimizing performance, consider cost implications. Some performance optimizations may have cost trade-offs, so strike a balance between performance and cost efficiency.

8.3 Cost Optimization Strategies

Effective cost optimization is a critical aspect of cloud management. While the cloud offers scalability and flexibility, it's essential to ensure that your cloud spending aligns with your organization's budget and objectives.

8.3.1 Cost Visibility and Governance

1. Cost Visibility: Gain visibility into your cloud costs by using cost management tools provided by your cloud provider or third-party solutions. These tools provide detailed insights into your spending patterns.

2. Budgeting: Set and monitor budgets for your cloud resources and projects. Budgets help you control spending and prevent unexpected cost overruns.

3. Cost Allocation: Implement cost allocation mechanisms to attribute costs to specific teams, projects, or departments. This enables cost accountability and transparency within your organization.

4. Governance Policies: Define governance policies that specify resource provisioning rules, access controls, and compliance requirements. Governance ensures that cloud resources are used efficiently and securely.

8.3.2 Rightsizing and Resource Optimization

1. Rightsizing: Continuously review the performance and utilization of your cloud resources. Rightsizing involves adjusting resource specifications to match the workload's actual requirements. Downsize underutilized resources and upgrade when necessary.

2. Auto-Scaling: Implement auto-scaling policies to automatically adjust resource capacity based on workload demands. This prevents overprovisioning during peak usage and reduces costs during idle periods.

3. Reserved Instances and Savings Plans: Leverage reserved instances (RIs) or savings plans provided by cloud providers. RIs offer substantial discounts in exchange for committing to a specific resource configuration for a defined period.

4. Resource Tagging: Use resource tagging to categorize and label cloud resources based on their purpose, owner, or project. Tagging simplifies cost allocation and tracking.

8.3.3 Cost Optimization Best Practices

1. Cloud-Native Services: Embrace cloud-native services and serverless computing to reduce infrastructure management overhead and optimize costs. Pay only for the resources and services you use.

2. Spot Instances: Consider using spot instances, if available in your cloud provider's offering, for non-critical workloads. Spot instances can provide significant cost savings but may be terminated with short notice.

3. Continuous Review: Regularly review your cloud environment for opportunities to optimize costs. Implement a process for periodic cost optimization assessments.

4. Monitoring and Alerts: Set up cost monitoring and alerting to be notified of unexpected spending increases. Promptly investigate and address cost anomalies.

5. Shutdown Policies: Implement policies to automatically shut down resources during non-business hours or when not in use. This is particularly useful for development and test environments.

6. Cost-Effective Storage: Optimize storage costs by selecting appropriate storage classes and archiving or deleting data that is no longer needed.

7. Cost Analysis Tools: Use cost analysis tools to identify trends, forecast future costs, and perform "what-if" scenarios to assess the impact of changes on your budget.

8. Cost Optimization Culture: Foster a culture of cost optimization within your organization. Educate teams on the importance of cost-conscious decisions and involve them in cost-saving initiatives.

8.4 Scaling Your Cloud Resources

One of the defining features of cloud computing is its ability to scale resources up or down based on demand. Effective resource scaling is crucial for maintaining optimal performance, managing costs, and delivering a seamless user experience.

8.4.1 Types of Scaling

1. Vertical Scaling (Scaling Up): Vertical scaling involves increasing the capacity of a single resource, such as upgrading the CPU, memory, or storage of a virtual machine. This approach is suitable for workloads that can be accommodated on a single, larger instance.

2. Horizontal Scaling (Scaling Out): Horizontal scaling involves adding more instances or resources to distribute the workload. It's a key strategy for achieving high availability, load balancing, and improved performance.

3. Auto-Scaling: Auto-scaling is an automated approach that dynamically adjusts the number of resources based on predefined criteria or metrics. It ensures that your application can handle fluctuating traffic without manual intervention.

8.4.2 Auto-Scaling Strategies

1. Load-Based Scaling: Implement load-based auto-scaling, where resources are added or removed based on metrics such as CPU utilization, network traffic, or application response times. Scaling policies define when and how resources are adjusted.

2. Scheduled Scaling: Use scheduled scaling to automatically adjust resources at predefined times or dates. This is useful for handling expected traffic patterns, such as scaling up during business hours and scaling down during off-peak periods.

3. Event-Driven Scaling: Implement event-driven scaling, which responds to specific events or triggers. For example, you can auto-scale in response to increased traffic, database query latency, or incoming messages.

4. Predictive Scaling: Utilize predictive scaling, where machine learning algorithms analyze historical data to forecast future resource needs. Predictive scaling can help prevent over-provisioning or under-provisioning.

8.4.3 Scaling Best Practices

1. Monitoring and Metrics: Establish comprehensive monitoring of your application and infrastructure. Use performance metrics to drive scaling decisions. Set up alerts to detect anomalies or performance bottlenecks.

2. Resource Templates: Create resource templates or use Infrastructure as Code (IaC) to ensure consistency when scaling resources. Templates simplify the provisioning process and reduce the risk of misconfigurations.

3. Graceful Scaling: Implement graceful scaling by gradually adding or removing resources to avoid sudden disruptions. Use techniques like blue-green deployments to minimize downtime during scaling operations.

4. Scaling Policies: Define clear and well-documented scaling policies that specify under what conditions resources should be scaled. Ensure that these policies align with your application's performance and availability requirements.

5. Cost Considerations: Consider the cost implications of scaling. While auto-scaling can improve performance, it can also increase costs. Set up budgets and cost controls to manage spending.

6. Load Balancers: Use load balancers to distribute incoming traffic evenly across multiple instances. Load balancing is essential for achieving high availability and scaling horizontally.

7. Test and Validation: Test your auto-scaling policies and procedures thoroughly. Verify that your application behaves as expected under various scaling scenarios.

8. Rolling Updates: If you need to deploy code changes during scaling operations, use rolling updates to ensure that updates are applied gradually without causing service disruptions.

9: CLOUD USE CASES AND CASE STUDIES

9.1 Cloud in Business and Industry

9.1.1 E-commerce and Retail

The e-commerce sector relies heavily on the cloud for its scalability and reliability. Retailers use cloud infrastructure to host their online stores, manage inventory, process transactions, and analyze customer data. The ability to auto-scale during peak shopping seasons ensures that e-commerce websites can handle high traffic loads, providing a seamless shopping experience.

9.1.2 Healthcare and Telemedicine

In healthcare, the cloud is instrumental in securely storing and managing electronic health records (EHRs) and medical data. Telemedicine platforms leverage the cloud to facilitate remote consultations and diagnostics, improving patient access to care. Cloud-based analytics enable medical researchers to process vast datasets for drug discovery and treatment development.

9.1.3 Finance and Fintech

The financial industry benefits from the cloud's speed and agility. Banks and financial institutions use cloud services for data analytics, fraud detection, and risk assessment. Fintech startups leverage the cloud to create innovative financial products, from digital wallets to peer-to-peer lending platforms.

9.1.4 Education and E-Learning

The education sector has witnessed a significant shift towards e-learning platforms hosted on the cloud. Educational institutions use cloud-based learning management systems (LMS) to deliver courses and content to students worldwide. Cloud resources support collaborative learning, data analysis, and online assessments.

9.1.5 Manufacturing and Industry 4.0

Manufacturers embrace the cloud to implement Industry 4.0 initiatives, which involve automation, data exchange, and smart manufacturing. Cloud-based Industrial Internet of Things (IIoT) platforms collect real-time data from sensors and machines, enabling predictive maintenance, quality control, and supply chain optimization.

9.1.6 Entertainment and Media

The entertainment industry relies on the cloud for content storage, distribution, and streaming. Video-on-demand (VoD) platforms use cloud infrastructure to deliver high-quality content to global audiences. Cloud-based rendering and special effects accelerate the production of movies and animations.

9.1.7 Startups and Innovation

Startups and small businesses leverage the cloud's cost-effectiveness and scalability to launch innovative products and services. Cloud services eliminate the need for substantial upfront investments in hardware and infrastructure, allowing startups to focus on product development and growth.

9.1.8 *Nonprofit and Humanitarian Efforts*

Cloud computing plays a crucial role in humanitarian efforts and nonprofit organizations. During crises, cloud resources provide the computing power needed for disaster response, data analysis, and communication. Nonprofits use the cloud to collaborate globally, manage donations, and raise awareness.

9.1.9 *Public Sector and Government*

Governments around the world are adopting cloud solutions to modernize their IT infrastructure, enhance citizen services, and improve data security. Cloud services enable government agencies to streamline operations, reduce costs, and increase transparency.

These examples illustrate the widespread influence of cloud computing across industries. The cloud's flexibility, scalability, and accessibility have empowered organizations to innovate, respond to market changes, and deliver value to customers and stakeholders in ways that were previously unimaginable.

9.2 Cloud in Education and Research

9.2.1 *Cloud-Powered Learning Environments*

1. Learning Management Systems (LMS): Educational institutions worldwide have adopted cloud-based Learning Management Systems (LMS) to deliver course content, facilitate online discussions, and track student progress. Cloud-hosted LMS platforms offer scalability, ensuring that institutions can accommodate growing numbers of students and courses.

2. Collaborative Tools: Cloud collaboration tools such as Google Workspace and Microsoft 365 have become essential for remote and blended learning environments. They enable students and educators to collaborate on projects, share documents, and conduct virtual meetings from anywhere with an internet connection.

3. Massive Open Online Courses (MOOCs): Cloud-based MOOC platforms like Coursera and edX provide access to high-quality educational content from top universities and institutions. These platforms leverage cloud scalability to serve millions of learners globally, democratizing education.

9.2.2 Cloud-Powered Research and Innovation

1. High-Performance Computing (HPC): Cloud providers offer HPC resources that empower researchers to perform complex simulations, data analysis, and scientific computations without the need for on-premises supercomputers. Cloud-based HPC accelerates research in fields such as genomics, climate modeling, and materials science.

2. Data Analytics and AI: Cloud-based data analytics and machine learning services enable researchers to analyze massive datasets, uncover insights, and develop predictive models. Cloud AI platforms provide pre-built machine learning models for various applications, from image recognition to natural language processing.

3. Data Sharing and Collaboration: Cloud storage and sharing solutions facilitate collaborative research across institutions and borders. Researchers can securely store and exchange datasets, research papers, and findings in the cloud, fostering global collaboration.

4. Virtual Labs: Cloud-powered virtual labs allow students and researchers to access and experiment with specialized equipment and software remotely. This approach broadens access to expensive or geographically distant resources, enhancing learning and research opportunities.

9.2.3 Case Study: Genomics Research Acceleration

One compelling case study in the realm of cloud-powered research is the field of genomics. Genomic research involves processing vast amounts of genetic data to understand diseases, track mutations, and develop personalized medicine. Traditional genomic analysis required dedicated on-premises infrastructure and substantial computing resources.

Cloud providers now offer genomics-specific solutions, such as Amazon Web Services (AWS) Genomics, Google Cloud Genomics, and Microsoft Genomics. These services allow researchers to analyze genomic data at scale, accelerating the pace of discovery. By leveraging the cloud's elasticity, genomics researchers can process data faster, share findings globally, and collaborate with other experts in the field.

The cloud's role in education and research extends beyond convenience; it's a catalyst for democratizing knowledge and accelerating breakthroughs. By providing access to advanced tools, resources, and collaboration opportunities, the cloud empowers students, educators, and researchers to push the boundaries of what's possible.

9.3 Cloud in Healthcare

9.3.1 Electronic Health Records (EHRs) and Interoperability

1. EHR Adoption: Healthcare providers are increasingly adopting cloud-based Electronic Health Records (EHR) systems. Cloud-hosted EHRs offer secure and accessible patient data storage, enabling healthcare professionals to access patient information from anywhere with an internet connection.

2. Interoperability: Cloud solutions promote interoperability by allowing different healthcare systems and providers to exchange patient data seamlessly. This interoperability improves care coordination, reduces duplication of tests, and enhances patient safety.

9.3.2 Telemedicine and Remote Patient Monitoring

1. Telemedicine Platforms: The cloud has fueled the rapid growth of telemedicine by providing secure and scalable platforms for remote consultations. Patients can connect with healthcare providers via video conferencing, improving access to care, especially in underserved areas.

2. Remote Monitoring: Cloud-enabled remote patient monitoring devices collect and transmit health data to healthcare providers in real time. This data helps in early detection of health issues, chronic disease management, and post-surgery care.

9.3.3 Medical Imaging and Diagnostics

1. PACS and Cloud Imaging: Picture Archiving and Communication Systems (PACS) in the cloud store and manage medical images such as X-rays, MRIs, and CT scans. Cloud PACS enhance image accessibility, enable remote consultations, and support rapid image analysis.

2. AI and Cloud Diagnostics: Cloud-based artificial intelligence (AI) algorithms analyze medical images and diagnostic data, assisting healthcare professionals in disease detection, treatment planning, and predictive analytics.

9.3.4 Healthcare Data Analytics and Research

1. Big Data Analytics: Cloud platforms provide the computational power and storage capacity needed for healthcare data analytics. Researchers can analyze large datasets to identify patterns, trends, and insights for drug discovery and epidemiological studies.

2. Genomic Medicine: Genomic research in healthcare relies on cloud computing for processing vast amounts of genetic data. Cloud-based genomic analysis accelerates personalized medicine, allowing tailored treatments based on individual genetic profiles.

9.3.5 Case Study: COVID-19 Pandemic Response

The COVID-19 pandemic showcased the vital role of cloud computing in healthcare. Cloud resources enabled rapid data sharing among researchers worldwide, facilitating the development of diagnostic tests, vaccines, and treatments. Telemedicine platforms supported remote consultations, reducing the risk of viral transmission in healthcare settings. Additionally, cloud-based contact tracing and epidemiological modeling assisted public health agencies in tracking the spread of the virus and making informed decisions.

The cloud's adoption in healthcare has not only improved patient care but also enabled innovation and collaboration across the industry. As healthcare providers continue to embrace cloud technologies, the potential for improved healthcare outcomes, cost savings, and medical breakthroughs remains limitless.

9.4 Real-world Cloud Case Studies

9.4.1 Case Study: Airbnb

Transforming Hospitality with Cloud Scalability

Overview: Airbnb, a global online marketplace for lodging and travel experiences, manages an enormous volume of data, from property listings to user reviews and bookings. To scale rapidly and meet increasing demand, Airbnb turned to the cloud.

Cloud Solution: Airbnb utilizes Amazon Web Services (AWS) to power its infrastructure. By leveraging AWS's elasticity and global reach, Airbnb can dynamically scale its resources based on user traffic, ensuring uninterrupted service even during peak booking periods.

Impact: The cloud has enabled Airbnb to expand globally, serving millions of hosts and travelers. It has also facilitated the development of innovative features like Smart Pricing and dynamic search capabilities. Airbnb's cloud-powered platform is a testament to how the cloud can support hyper-growth in the sharing economy.

9.4.2 Case Study: NASA Jet Propulsion Laboratory (JPL)

Exploring the Cosmos with Cloud Data

Overview: NASA's Jet Propulsion Laboratory (JPL) manages complex missions exploring the solar system and beyond. JPL collects vast amounts of telemetry and scientific data from spacecraft, rovers, and satellites.

Cloud Solution: JPL utilizes Google Cloud Platform (GCP) for data storage, analysis, and collaboration. Cloud resources enable scientists to process and analyze data from multiple missions, including the Mars rovers and the Juno spacecraft.

Impact: The cloud has revolutionized space exploration by providing efficient data storage and processing capabilities. JPL scientists can collaborate globally, share findings, and make discoveries more rapidly. Cloud technology plays a crucial role in advancing our understanding of the cosmos.

9.4.3 Case Study: Netflix

Entertainment on a Global Scale with Cloud Streaming

Overview: Netflix, the world's leading streaming platform, serves millions of viewers with a vast library of movies and TV shows. To deliver content seamlessly worldwide, Netflix relies on cloud infrastructure.

Cloud Solution: Netflix relies heavily on Amazon Web Services (AWS) for content delivery, database management, and analytics. AWS's global network of data centers ensures low-latency streaming for viewers in different regions.

Impact: The cloud has allowed Netflix to scale its streaming service globally, expand its content library, and provide personalized recommendations. Netflix's success demonstrates how cloud technology can revolutionize the entertainment industry and reshape how we consume content.

9.4.4 Case Study: Lyft

Ride-Sharing Reinvented with Cloud Data Insights

Overview: Lyft, a leading ride-sharing platform, collects a wealth of data on drivers, passengers, routes, and pricing. To optimize its services and enhance rider experiences, Lyft relies on cloud-based data analytics.

Cloud Solution: Lyft leverages Google Cloud Platform (GCP) for data storage and analysis. GCP's BigQuery and machine learning tools enable Lyft to gain insights into driver behavior, demand patterns, and route optimization.

Impact: The cloud has empowered Lyft to improve driver efficiency, reduce wait times for riders, and enhance safety measures. It exemplifies how data-driven insights derived from cloud analytics can drive innovation in the sharing economy.

These case studies demonstrate the versatility of cloud computing in different industries. From hospitality to space exploration, entertainment to transportation, organizations leverage the cloud to scale, innovate, and deliver exceptional value to their customers and stakeholders. These real-world examples underscore the transformative power of cloud technology.

10: ETHICAL CONSIDERATIONS IN CLOUD COMPUTING

The adoption of cloud computing has brought about remarkable technological advancements and opportunities. However, with great power comes great responsibility. Ethical considerations in cloud computing are essential to ensure that technology is used in ways that are fair, just, and responsible.

Data Privacy and Security

Data privacy is one of the foremost ethical concerns in cloud computing. Organizations and cloud providers must ensure that user data is handled with the utmost care and in compliance with privacy regulations such as the General Data Protection Regulation (GDPR) and the California Consumer Privacy Act (CCPA). Mishandling or unauthorized access to sensitive data can result in privacy breaches, identity theft, and loss of trust.

Ethical Considerations:

- **Informed Consent:** Cloud users must be fully informed about how their data will be collected, used, and protected. Obtaining clear and explicit consent is crucial.

- **Data Encryption:** Ensuring data is encrypted both in transit and at rest is a fundamental practice in safeguarding user privacy.
- **Data Ownership:** Clarifying data ownership and control is essential. Users should have the ability to access, modify, or delete their data as needed.

Bias and Fairness in AI

Artificial Intelligence (AI) algorithms, often employed in cloud-based services, have the potential to perpetuate biases present in historical data. Biased AI systems can lead to unfair outcomes, especially in decision-making processes related to lending, hiring, and criminal justice. Addressing bias and promoting fairness in AI is an ethical imperative.

Ethical Considerations:

- **Bias Mitigation:** Developers must actively work to identify and mitigate bias in AI algorithms, ensuring that they do not discriminate against specific groups.
- **Algorithm Transparency:** AI models should be transparent, explainable, and accountable, allowing users to understand how decisions are made.
- **Auditing AI:** Periodic audits of AI systems should be conducted to detect and rectify bias and unfairness.

Environmental Impact

Cloud computing, while enabling efficiency and scalability, also has environmental implications. Data centers that power the cloud consume vast amounts of energy, contributing to carbon emissions and environmental degradation. Ethical cloud providers are increasingly adopting sustainable practices and renewable energy sources to reduce their carbon footprint.

Ethical Considerations:

- **Sustainable Practices:** Cloud providers should prioritize energy efficiency and sustainable data center designs.
- **Renewable Energy:** Transitioning to renewable energy sources, such as solar and wind power, is a responsible choice for cloud providers.
- **Carbon Offsetting:** Some cloud providers invest in carbon offset programs to mitigate the environmental impact of their operations.

Vendor Lock-In and Interoperability

Vendor lock-in, where organizations become heavily dependent on a particular cloud provider's services, can limit choice and flexibility. Ethical concerns arise when a lack of interoperability prevents data and applications from being easily transferred between cloud platforms.

Ethical Considerations:

- **Interoperability Standards:** Encouraging the development of industry-wide interoperability standards can prevent vendor lock-in and promote choice.
- **Data Portability:** Organizations should have the ability to move their data and applications between cloud providers without significant barriers.
- **Transparency in Contracts:** Cloud service agreements should be transparent and fair, ensuring that organizations understand the terms and consequences of vendor lock-in.

Addressing these ethical considerations requires collaboration among cloud providers, regulatory bodies, and users. Ethical cloud computing practices are essential not only to protect user rights and privacy but also to ensure the responsible and sustainable growth of cloud technology.

11: CLOUD COMPUTING CERTIFICATION AND TRAINING

As cloud computing continues to evolve and play an increasingly significant role in the IT industry, individuals and organizations are recognizing the importance of acquiring the skills and knowledge necessary to leverage cloud technologies effectively. Cloud computing certification and training programs have emerged as valuable resources to help individuals enhance their expertise and validate their proficiency in this field.

Why Pursue Cloud Computing Certification?

Certifications in cloud computing offer several benefits, including:

1. **Validation of Expertise:** Cloud certifications demonstrate to employers and peers that you possess the knowledge and skills required to work with cloud technologies effectively.
2. **Career Advancement:** Earning a cloud certification can open up new career opportunities and increase your earning potential in the IT industry.
3. **Stay Current:** Cloud certifications often require ongoing education and recertification, ensuring that professionals stay up-to-date with the latest cloud trends and technologies.

4. **Industry Recognition:** Many certifications are recognized and respected across the IT industry, providing a universally accepted credential.

Here are some popular cloud computing certifications and the skills they validate:

1. AWS Certified Solutions Architect

- **Skills Validated:** Designing and deploying scalable, highly available, and fault-tolerant systems on Amazon Web Services (AWS).
- **Certification Provider:** Amazon Web Services (AWS)

2. Microsoft Certified: Azure Administrator Associate

- **Skills Validated:** Managing Azure resources, implementing and managing virtual networks, and securing identities in Azure.
- **Certification Provider:** Microsoft Azure

3. Google Cloud Professional Cloud Architect

- **Skills Validated:** Designing, developing, and managing Google Cloud solutions, ensuring reliability, security, and scalability.
- **Certification Provider:** Google Cloud

4. Certified Cloud Security Professional (CCSP)

- **Skills Validated:** Cloud security, risk management, compliance, and governance in cloud environments.
- **Certification Provider:** (ISC)^2

5. Certified Kubernetes Administrator (CKA)

- **Skills Validated:** Proficiency in Kubernetes container orchestration and management.

- **Certification Provider:** Cloud Native Computing Foundation (CNCF)

6. CompTIA Cloud+

- **Skills Validated:** Cloud computing concepts, virtualization, infrastructure, security, and troubleshooting.
- **Certification Provider:** CompTIA

7. Certified Cloud Practitioner

- **Skills Validated:** Foundational knowledge of AWS cloud services, architecture, pricing, and compliance.
- **Certification Provider:** Amazon Web Services (AWS)

Training and Study Resources

Preparing for cloud computing certification exams often involves self-study, instructor-led training, or a combination of both. Here are some valuable resources to aid in your certification journey:

- **Online Courses:** Platforms like Coursera, edX, Udemy, and Pluralsight offer a wide range of cloud computing courses, including exam-specific preparation courses.
- **Official Documentation:** Cloud providers such as AWS, Microsoft Azure, and Google Cloud offer comprehensive documentation and whitepapers to help candidates understand their services and best practices.
- **Practice Exams:** Many certification providers offer practice exams or sample questions to help you assess your readiness.
- **Books:** There are numerous books and study guides available for various cloud certifications.
- **Certification Prep Workshops:** Consider attending workshops or training sessions conducted by certified instructors or training organizations.
- **Hands-On Labs:** Practical experience with cloud services is crucial. Cloud providers often offer free tiers for hands-on practice.

Choosing the Right Certification

When selecting a cloud computing certification, consider your career goals, current skills, and the cloud platform you or your organization primarily use. Each certification caters to specific roles and expertise levels, so it's essential to align your choice with your professional aspirations.

Whether you're looking to become a cloud architect, a cloud security expert, a developer, or an administrator, cloud computing certifications provide a structured path to acquiring the knowledge and skills required for success in the cloud-centric IT landscape.